Alchemical
Musings

Alchemical Musings

Ralph Metzner

Four Trees Press

*COVER: The alchemical masculine and feminine aspects of nature,
mixing chemicals in the vessel (within) until finally the sun, the power of
transmutation, bearing the golden flower, appears.*

Printed in the U.S.A.

FOUR TREES PRESS
PO Box 692
El Verano, CA 95433
www.FourTreesPress.com

Contents

Foreword

Ralph Metzner first wrote about alchemy when he was in his early 30s. He included a chapter on alchemy in his book *Maps of Consciousness*, which was published in 1971. As a professor at the California Institute of Integral Studies, he taught a course titled "Alchemy and Depth Psychology," as part of the East-West Psychology Program. The study of alchemy was also a part of a course he taught on esoteric systems of thought. I was a student in his alchemy class in the summer of 1983, as well as of the esoteric systems course during the academic year. In the 1990s he wrote about a process he called *Alchemical Divination*, and developed that into a training program which he taught for more than a decade in the early 2000s. In the latter few years of his life he recorded his thoughts on some 36 alchemical terms. Over an arc of some 50 years, Ralph worked on the practice of using alchemical processes for inner transformation. This volume of alchemical musings combines his earliest writing on alchemy with his last writings on alchemical terms.

A week before Ralph died, he met with his editor/ book agent and me, his once graduate student, partner, and wife of 30 years, and asked us to publish the alchemical terms if he died before he got them published. After reading the alchemical word descriptions, I thought of combining them with his early book chapter on alchemy. I have woven the terms through the alchemy text where they fit in with the narrative *(in italics)*.

Ralph developed his own connection to alchemy first through an embodied practice of light fire-yoga called Agni Yoga. He worked with the concepts of alchemy in his everyday self-observation and in his work with students and clients that often included, in addition to Agni Yoga, working with altered states of consciousness, including psychedelics, which he notes in the text as "the new alchemy."

Ralph's pathways working with agni yoga, astrology, transpersonal psychology, and psychedelics informed his experiential connection to the felt field of the psyche and its healing properties. In these pages of musings on alchemy, you can see Ralph at work on his calling and interests as he differentiates from Jung and others in this tradition.

In the text Ralph describes the high quality character, devotion, and sincerity required of the alchemist. He notes that the alchemist honors the *natura naturans* (L.), that nature is doing everything naturally, and offering core guidance. The alchemist regarded alchemy as a sacred art, while at the same time was concerned about the animal aspects of human nature. Having lived with him for 33 years, I can attest that Ralph embodied the qualities of the alchemist in his daily life.

You are extended a warm invitation to explore the alchemical musings and metaphors in this volume that bookends his adult lifetime. This work combines his early thought with his last years of wisdom and expertise. While this is a collection of musings rather than a complete, coherent text on alchemy, it is a sort of alchemical transmutation of his lifelong opus into gold.

– Cathy Coleman
July 27, 2019
Sonoma, California

PART ONE
ALCHEMY

The Chemistry of Inner Union

Turn inward for your voyage! For all your arts
You will not find the Stone in foreign parts.
—Angelus Silesius

The history of alchemy is intimately connected with the history of the so-called secret societies of the European Middle Ages. The secrecy of these groups was in part a political survival necessity. Their teachings, which involved liberation from false concepts and pre-programmed designs, if openly declared, would have aroused the opposition of the established church. In part, also, the need for secrecy is inherent in the nature of the work of schools of inner transformation. It is the secrecy of a technical language, not the secrecy of an attempt to gain political or commercial advantage, although this was precisely the accusation leveled against them.

The secrecy factor makes it difficult to reconstruct the history of these psychological schools with any accuracy, especially since much of the information about them derives from the defamatory distortions of the churchly opposition. It seems reasonably certain though that throughout that period when Europe was dominated by the power of the church these schools of psychological transformation continued to arise. To what extent there was an unbroken continuity of tradition, reappearing in different guises, and to what extent new teachings were formulated in concepts derived from ancient, semi-mythical sources in order to facilitate their acceptance, is difficult to say. The alchemists and other groups tended to emphasize that their teaching was the same as that taught by the "ancient sages": the first teacher was always Hermes Trismegistos, an Egyptian initiate, whom Egyptians identified with Thoth, the scribe of the gods, and the Greeks identified with Hermes, the messenger of the gods. Numerous works of anonymous medieval Latin alchemists were simply attributed to Hermes. Other ancients, whom the alchemists cited as initiates in their tradition, include Solomon, Pythagoras, Socrates, Plato, and Anaxagoras; and among medievalists, Avicenna, Albertus Magnus, Roger Bacon, Raymond Lully, and others.

The pattern observable in this tradition is somewhat as follows: the initial school or college of adepts is established, teaching the techniques of transformation and the associated knowledge of man's psychophysiological constitution. Around a nucleus of usually anonymous teachers grows a community or brotherhood, which, in order to exemplify and externalize the teachings and at the same time generate the material resources to support itself, specializes in one or another of the arts or sciences. Thus the Freemasons were originally a group of adepts who were also master architects and builders, and who studied the laws of geometry and proportion and the nature of materials in order to build temples which would inspire and raise the consciousness even of those who knew nothing of their purpose.[1]

Others, such as the Rosicrucians (the Brothers of the Cross of the Rose) and the Brotherhood of the Golden Cross, specialized in the natural sciences and studied the workings of God and Nature in the cosmos (astrology) and in the composition of matter (alchemy). Yet others investigated herbs and pharmacy and developed new approaches to medicine and healing. The seventeenth-century German alchemist Paracelsus, for example, was the first to develop the concept of chemical specificity, still one of the cornerstones of modern therapeutics. The Knights Templar, which probably began as an attempt by a group of adepts who were members of the military caste to convert the warriors to a spiritual orientation, channeled their external activities into commerce and cultural exchange, and were responsible for bringing much material and scientific wealth to the West from the Arabic and Greek worlds.

The commonly accepted view of alchemy among contemporary scientists is that though their researchers had the merit of paving the way for the development of modern chemistry, yet they were regrettably steeped in the useless and superstitious quest to make gold. This despite the repeated and insistent statements of the alchemists that *aurum nostrum non est aurum vulgum,* "our gold is not the common gold," and that "our" mercury is not the common mercury. Thus, the anonymous author of an alchemical tract titled "An

Open Entrance to the Closed Palace of the King" says: "I have spoken about mercury, sulphur, the vessel, the treatment, etc.,—and of course, all these things are to be understood with a grain of salt. You must understand . . . that I have spoken metaphorically; if you take my words literally you will reap no harvest."[2]

Here, and elsewhere, it is clearly stated that the language of chemistry employed by the alchemists is a metaphor for the inner work, the opus, of psychic transformation. The transmutation of "base metals" into "gold" is the transmutation of psychophysical elements within man from an impure, obstructed state to a fine state of responsiveness to high-frequency energy. The precious metals were regarded as the most evolved members of the mineral kingdom; so, by analogy, to "make gold" by "our art" was to make oneself into a more highly evolved member of the human kingdom.

Opus (L.) – ("the work"). The work of self-transformation, on the physical, perceptual, emotional, and mental dimensions of consciousness. The process of self-transformation to higher consciousness does not happen accidentally or spontaneously by itself — although there may be unexpected peak experiences, or moments of "gratuitous grace." But for ongoing radical self-transformation towards higher consciousness, we need intention and we need practice, which is, of course, a creative work. In the realm of musical creation, "opus" is used to designate the sequence of a composer's creative output, arranged in chronological order. In the alchemical opus of self-transformation we are both the composer and the performer – and the processes we engage in are arrayed along the time-line of our lives. So the opus *of our youthful years may be decidedly different than the* opus *of our later years.*

Opus contra naturam (L.) *This is a second core motto of the alchemical work: "working against nature" refers to conscious intentional work against the inertial pull of unconscious habits. This is a core principle of practice in "fourth way" teachings such as those of Zen Buddhism, Sufism, Gurdjieff and others.*

And this was not an exclusive, separative endeavor: when the alchemists say "our gold" they do not mean ours as opposed to yours, but the gold that is within us, as opposed to the gold of the goldsmiths. There is in the writings of the alchemists an intense, almost poignant ambivalence between their desire to share the valuable knowledge and art they have learned and the knowledge that this sharing is possible only to a very limited degree, because of the possible danger both to the art and the individual, if premature information came into the wrong hands. "For the matter is so glorious and wonderful that it cannot be fully delivered to anyone but by word of mouth."[3]

The genuine alchemical adepts were aware, of course, that their teachings were being distorted and abused by charlatans who claimed to be able to make physical gold, and who preyed on the concupiscence of the ignorant. They denounced the "huffers and puffers" who said they could "multiply metals"; and pointed out, quite logically, that if these imposters really were able to make gold, they wouldn't be wandering around boasting of it, and "cheating the credulous out of their money." Yet their protestations were in vain, and the low reputation, which alchemy acquired as the result of the activities of fraudulent imitators, has prevailed to this day.

Although modern scientists accuse the alchemists of trying to make money, and believe that by pursuing science for its own sake they have arrived at a more exact and comprehensive knowledge, this is actually a quite false and idealized picture. The majority of modern scientists work for industry and government, for money; the determination of the goal or purpose of the scientific experimentation is often left to politicians and businessmen. Consequently, the researches of modern chemists and physicists, originally started by alchemists as an aid to man's own evolution, have become quite separated from this purpose. Using chemistry to make money, which is what the alchemists were accused of trying to do, is what the modern chemists and their patrons actually do.

In modern times the study of alchemy has received a new infusion of interest due to the work of Carl Jung. In his autobiography, Jung relates how during a period of several years in the middle of his life, he was exposed to a "confrontation with the unconscious," that is, images, dreams, and fantasies which were both very strange and very powerful, rose up uncontrollably into his awareness. He had a dream in which he felt that he was "caught in the seventeenth century." Soon be began to notice that "analytical psychology coincided in a curious way with alchemy."[4] The dream symbols and images he encountered had numerous parallels in the alchemical literature. This discovery was extremely important to Jung because it indicated to him that the psychic experiences he was undergoing were not purely personal-subjective, but had collective, historical antecedents. Jung had no external teacher or companion explorers with whom to verify his experiences, and he found himself in an extremely isolated position without such external confirmation. For this reason, Jung regarded his work in alchemy as that which gave his psychology "its place in reality and established [it] upon its historical foundations."[5]

Jung made pioneering advances in recognizing the importance of the alchemical tradition and its continued relevance to modern man's quest for self-understanding and individuation, yet he was not able to step outside the role of the scholar. "I worked along philological lines, as if I were trying to solve the riddle of an unknown language."[6] The actual experimental practice of the art of alchemy eluded him, because, as they themselves repeatedly said, this could only be taught by word of mouth, by a teacher. In this way, despite his sincere and persevering efforts in the realm of scholarship, Jung fell victim to the inherent trap of the intellectual approach: that of assuming that mental knowledge is true understanding. Hence he accuses the alchemists of "incredible naiveté," in projecting their fantasies into matter; although the contradiction between this and the great psychological wisdom with which he credits them, seems to escape him. A mere projection of fantasies into matter would not have lasted a thousand years with such profound effects on all areas of European life and culture.

Jung's blind spot regarding the role of the body led him to miss the point that the transmutation of substances took place within the psychophysical organism, even when the alchemists say this explicitly. Thus, when Paracelsus says, "The microcosm in its interior anatomy must be reverberated up to the highest reverberation," Jung interprets this as, "While the artifex heats the chemical substance in the furnace he himself is morally undergoing the same fiery torment and purification."[7] Yet Paracelsus is quite literally referring to an actual process of raising the vibratory rate of structures in the "interior anatomy" by means of "fire" ("reverberation is ignition"). It is not just a "projection" of "moral" purification, or becoming "unconsciously identical" with a process going on in an external furnace, as Jung would have it.

Perhaps this difference of interpretation can best be made clear by relating a personal experience. A short while after having begun to study the Yoga of Fire, which has many points in common with the alchemical work, I interrupted a yoga session in order to brew myself a cup of tea. While waiting for the water to boil, I sat down in the kitchen and continued to work with the "fire." Shortly I became aware of the sound of the water beginning to heat up. As I was attempting to increase the heat of the inner fire, a linkage was spontaneously set up between the internal and the external heating. When the water reached the boiling point, there was a definite discontinuous energy change internally, experienced subjectively as a kind of release. In other words, the external heating provided a kind of support to the inner work, akin to the role of *mandala* in visual meditation. There was no projection of images, or identification going on here; I was fully aware of both processes and the difference between them.

This experience suggested to me that where the alchemists actually employed physical apparatus in their experiments, which was not necessarily very often, they were perhaps working with this type of procedure. They might have been setting up laboratory analogues of internal transformation processes, and using these analogues as supports for inner work. In the text entitled "The Sophic Hydrolith, or Water-Stone of the Wise," there is a passage which seems to refer to this procedure: "We saw that in our chemical operation the regulation of the fire, and a most patient and careful tempering of its heat, was of the greatest importance . . . we also spoke of the 'fire of the Sages' as being one of the chief agents in our chemical process, and said that it was an essential, preternatural and Divine fire, that it lay hid in our substance, and that it was stirred into action by the influence and aid of the outward, material fire."[8]

Another author makes careful distinction between the "truly secret furnace, which a vulgar eye never saw," and the "common furnace, made of potter's earth."[9] One of the essential requirements of the latter was that "you must be able to keep up in it a fire for ten or twelve hours, without looking to it"; which suggests that it was used as an external support to the inner or "living fire" that burns in "our vessel."

The evolution of awareness, in seven stages from the fixed plant stage to the mobile human being stage, through the transforming power of lightning-fire.

The alchemists were adepts first and natural scientists second. That is, their goal and purpose and main endeavor was evolutionary transformation of man's total being. Their methods were taught by direct contact between teacher and student. Yet they believed that since man is a microcosm, the processes they observed and studied internally could also be found externally, in Nature, and vice versa. "If, therefore, we wish to exercise the fine Art of Alchemy, we must imitate the method by which Nature does her work in bowels of the earth."[10] Alchemical texts are laboratory manuals for the great experiment of Nature, which we carry out in our own nature: self-transformation.

It is impossible at this date to determine to what extent actual physical experimental setups were used by the alchemical adepts. Many were evidently distressed at and disapproving of an increasing trend to use external materials. One author, quoting Nature, writes: "Let me tell you that your artificial fire will never impart my heavenly warmth."[11] And continues later: "All you want is leisure, and some place where you can be without any fear of interruptions." Another author emphasizes: "There is but one vessel, one method, and one consummation."[12] Yet another implores: "Relinquish the multiplicity of methods and substances, for our substance is one." Clearly, the setting up of laboratory analogues as aids established a tendency for some of the alchemists to concern themselves more and more with the nature and composition of external elements and thus lose track of the original goal. This is essentially the birth of modern chemistry, which, in the course of time, then proliferated into numberless specialized subdisciplines.

The alchemists often referred to their method as the "spagyric" art, a compound word made from Greek roots meaning "to take apart" and "to bring together." Thus it was a combination of what is today called analytic and synthetic chemistry, in the interior sphere: the separation of elements, the extraction of gold from ore, on the one hand, and the synthesis of finer substances, the combining of elements, on the other. Analysis probes, goes into, takes apart: it is a masculine, dynamic function. Synthesis contains, combines, encloses: it is a feminine, magnetic function. The fusion of male and female energies, known as the conjunction, is the central process of alchemy. Many of the illustrations of the work show a man on the left and a woman on the right performing various operations in the vessel, in the center. They are preparing what was called "the chemical wedding," the marriage of chemicals within.

Coniunctio (L.) - ("conjunction"). The conjoining, connecting or unifying of two disparate states or processes, weaving together two separate entities or patterns into a new, stronger, healthier wholeness.

In astronomy and astrology, two or more planets or points are said to be conjunct *when they occupy the same degree of longitude in the zodiac. The Sun and Moon, which symbolize the masculine and feminine in astrology, are* conjunct *at the New Moon.*

In psychophysical yogic alchemy, coniunctio *refers to practices of balancing the dynamic and receptive poles of the multidimensional human energy field. This field is a polarized electromagnetic antenna system, also called the aura, for receiving and transmitting energies of diverse vibrational frequencies in the multiple worlds of reality and consciousness. Whether clothed in the body of a man or woman the Immortal Spirit and Soul of every human is androgynous.*

At the psychophysical and personality levels, the human being manifests as one or the other, male or female, with in-between variations produced by epigenetic, embryonic and fetal conditions. The conjoining *and integration of the masculine animus and feminine anima is the key central process of psychophysical alchemy. One example of* coniunctio *symbolism in alchemical illustrations is images of a hermaphroditic human being — male on the left side and female on the right. Similar images exist in Indian tantric art. This can be seen as a portrayal of the* coniunctio *practice of visualizing the right side of one's body as male and the left side as female.*

The classic Indian yoga posture of sitting cross-legged with hands linked in the lap can also be seen as the portrayal of a coniunctio *practice: the two poles, dynamic and magnetic, are turned inward and balanced along the central axis, rather than being outwardly oriented, as they are in the normal waking state consciousness and in the activities of daily living.*

The hermetic vessel, called by some "the root and the principle of our art," that in which all the operations of alchemy are performed, is the human body, or rather the whole organization of bodies and fields considered under the aspect of regenerative inner work. Jung writes: "The Hermetic vessel is a uterus of spiritual renewal or rebirth"[13]; and this is half the picture. For the renewal is physical as well as spiritual. The vessel is said to be circular, or egg-shaped, corresponding to the shape of the organizing field seen by sensitives around human beings. The use of the word *vessel* recalls early Christian mystics who saw the body as the "vessel of the spirit," in which the "second birth" of the regeneration takes place. The alchemical "Liber Quartorum"

("Book of the Four") says, "like the work of God is the vessel of the divine seed, for it has received the clay, moulded it, and mixed it with fire and water."[14] The rebirth of the new man, or second Adam, following the work of regeneration through fusion of male and female (sometimes called the spagyric birth) brings forth the son of the wise, that is the actual, knowing Self, the hermaphroditic One, the unified being.

For the proper mixing of chemicals to take place the alchemists emphasized the importance of keeping the vessel sealed. This so-called hermetic seal is like a protective field which the adept establishes around himself, to prevent "air" from coming in, that is, extraneous thought-forms which could be destructive to the process, as well as to prevent "air" from leaking out, that is, to prevent mental energy being dissipated in outward projections. This latter aspect recalls Patanjali's definition of yoga as "the restriction of the fluctuations of mind-stuff."

The Four Elements

Central to the thinking of the alchemical philosophers is the idea that macrocosmic Nature and man, the microcosm, are made up of the four elements: fire, air, water, and earth. This notion is not at all far-fetched when it is remembered that 99 percent of the atoms of proteins, the chief ingredient of living matter, are constituted of the elements carbon, oxygen, hydrogen, and nitrogen. Perhaps this is one aspect of what the alchemists meant by the four elements.

Another aspect is what we nowadays call the states of matter. Molecules bound into relatively fixed, immobile structures are solid; within the body, bones, muscles, cartilage, connective tissue, and cell structures are the "earth elements" of our nature. The alchemists say: "Elementary earth is like a sponge, and the receptacle of all other elements."[15]

With a rise in temperature the movement of molecules in a substance increases and matter enters the liquid state; our organism is 70 percent liquid, with its circulating blood and lymph systems, hormones, and intracellular fluids. The alchemists refer to this fluid medium of life as the *aqua permanens*, the "permanent water," or as *mare nostrum*, "our sea." Through its connection with the endocrine system, "water" is associated with the emotional nature. The bloodstream, it has been said by Rodney Collin, is "an index of a man's being."[16]

The gaseous state of matter is marked by still higher temperatures and degree of activity; the molecules are in ceaseless, random motion. The alchemists said air "contains the vital spirit of all creatures . . . it nourishes, impregnates, conserves the other elements."[17] It is hardly necessary to point out that the consistent oxygenation of blood is a vital part of the continuing life process, and particularly of cerebral processes. Or, as the alchemists put it, "We see that water becomes foul and unwholesome without a supply of fresh air."

The breath of life is the carrier of energy in the process of creation, as God breathed life into the form of Adam; it is also intimately involved in all systems of yogic regeneration, or re-creation, and metaphorically, we find it in the "inspiration" of artistic creativity. The very words *spirit* and *psyche* come from Greek and Latin words meaning "to breathe." In most esoteric philosophy and in the symbolism of many dreams and fantasies, "air" is associated with the thinking nature, the "wings of thought."

The statements of the alchemists concerning fire are less easily interpreted in terms of states of matter. Knowing what we do now about the electromagnetic wave properties of matter, and the interchangeability of the wave-energy aspect and particle-matter aspect, one could say that electricity is a fourth state of matter, and identify it with the sensory-perceptual nervous system in the body, which functions electrically. However, the alchemists either did not possess this information or did not write about it; they were concerned mostly with fire in its aspect of purifying energy.

"Would you know the perfect Master?" asks "The Ordinal of Alchemy." "It is he who understands the regulation of the fire, and its degrees."[18] The author goes on to describe thirteen different kinds of fire and when to use them. Another text, entitled "The Glory of the World," states that "without this fire our Art cannot be brought to a successful issue. . . . It is the most precious fire that God has created in the earth and has a thousand virtues. . . . It has the purifying virtue of Purgatory."[19] Yet others identify fire with spirit or soul. Although sometimes the alchemists identify their "fire of the Sages,"

The salamander as the spirit of the living fire. This is the reiteration, gradation, and amelioration of the Philosophers' Stone; the whole is called its augmentation.

with the fire of hell or purgatory, when describing its purifying aspects, yet mostly they emphasize that the art is to be carried out with "gentle cooking."

Yet another aspect of the doctrine of the four elements is that this may be a metaphor for the subtle bodies which we encounter in all esoteric philosophy. These bodies are held to differ in material density, or in frequency of vibration. The earth body, which is the one we perceive with our physical senses, is the densest, and has the lowest frequency. "Water" then refers to the emotional body, also known as the astral body. This is a different level of consciousness which links into but is not identical with the fluid components of the physical, earth body. Similarly, "air" refers then to the mental body, also known as the causal body, the mental level of consciousness, which links into but is not identical with the brain systems.

Elemental Air. One of the traditional four elements that are the mythopoetic foundation of the Graeco-Roman worldview in the pre-scientific era is elemental air. A residue of this correspondence in scientific and everyday languages is the term atmosphere – the sphere of atmos (Greek "vapor" or "breath").

At the planetary level, elemental air *corresponds to winds, clouds and all atmospheric phenomena. Winds are the breathing of planet Earth, vitalizing and refreshing all plant and animal life.*

In esoteric teachings there are four levels of consciousness, called "sheaths" or "bodies" of differing density. The least dense of these is the mental level, also called noetic (Greek noesis, "knowing").

In Jung's psychology the teaching of four aspects of the psyche appears in his theory of four functions and four types, with air *symbolizing the thinking function and the type in which that function predominates. "Wings of thought" is an expression that reflects that association. "Wind-bag" and "blow-hard" are colloquial expressions suggesting imbalanced emphasis on* air *and mind in communication.*

At the human level, air *is the basis and medium*

for breathing, speaking and singing, associated with the energy centers and organs of the head, throat and thoracic cavity.

Colloquially, a scene or a person may bring us a "breath of fresh air", especially welcome when we are bored or tired. We may be left "breathless with awe" at the sudden appearance of beauty in a person, a performance or a natural landscape. We may speak or hear in a "whisper," conveying either loving intimacy, or malicious gossip. We may recognize an individual or work of art as "inspiring" or "inspired" – metaphorically as coming from the in-breathing of creative genius.

A proverbial expression alluding to impractical fantasizing is "building castles in the air". In Shakespeare's Twelfth Night, alluding to the echoing effect of air, one of the characters says "Halloo your name to the reverberate hills and make the babbling gossip of the air cry out". And in Shakespeare's Tempest, the wizard Prospero asserts the final unreality of creative imaginings when he says, "Our revels now are ended. These our actors ... were all spirits, and are melted into air, into thin air — like the baseless fabric of this vision."

Elemental Water. At the planetary level, the element water *corresponds to oceans, tides, lakes, rivers, springs, pools and rain. Three-fourths of the Earth's surface is covered in* water. *An evolutionary systems cosmology based on the work of Vladimir Vernadsky and Teilhard de Chardin proposes a system of concentric spheres around a fiery core — the lithosphere as the sphere of rock, hydrosphere* *as the sphere of* water, *atmosphere as the sphere of air, and the biosphere as the sphere of life.*

Three-fourths of the mass of the human body is fluid and life on Earth is a water-based *system. The salty chemistry of blood resembles that of sea*water. *Biological tides ebb and flow through the bodies of all animals and plants, in synchrony with the ocean tides, pulled by lunar and solar gravity.*

Analogically, rivers and lakes correspond to the arteries, blood vessels, lymph and endocrine systems of the body and rain to the fertilizing moisturizing of hormones and sexual fluids. Elemental water *is associated with feelings and emotions and the energy centers of the chest and solar plexus. Alchemists used the expressions* aqua permanens, *"permanent* water," *and* mare nostrum, *"our sea," to refer to the* watery, *fluid components of our being.*

Numerous colloquial expressions refer to symbolic associations, both positive and negative, between emotions and fluids. We may experience tears of joy and tears of sorrow. We may recognize someone bubbling infectiously with happiness and joy, or dampening our fiery enthusiasm. Someone may be a like a wet blanket at a party or social gathering, or stimulating laughter in everyone to the point of tears, or wishy-washy in their indecisiveness. One may shrug off the negative judgments of others like water *off a duck's back. And we may appreciate a sad blues song that sings of drowning in my own tears.*

We recognize a deep psychological truth in the traditional saying that "you can lead a horse to the water, *but you can't make him drink." Shakespeare refers to the important difference between surface feeling and depth of emotions, when a character in Henry VI, says "smooth runs the water when the brook is deep." Here too, the meaning is both positive and negative: the surface may be calm but conceal hidden rocks or dangerous cross-currents.*

Elemental Fire. In the pre-scientific, earth-centered world view of ancient and medieval times in Europe fire was one of the traditional four elements that constituted all of reality, along with air, water and earth. The modern scientific worldview recognizes an evolving and expanding list of some 118 fundamental elements, with known

Union of Fire and Water.

atomic structure. In addition it recognizes the fiery core of planetary structure, which science has penetrated only to a limited extent.

The four elements remain as colloquial symbols in literature and everyday language. The traditional symbolism of fire *extends to terrestrial* fires *such as lightning, erupting volcanoes, and forest* fires. *More broadly it includes all forms of radiant energy, along the entire electro-magnetic spectrum, cosmic radiation, and various forms of bio-electricity.*

In the human organism, fire *is experienced as bodily heat and vitality, the electro-chemical activity of the nervous systems and bio-electrical fields involved in healing and regeneration. This includes the various formulations of subtle life-energy processes, such as chi, prana, kundalini, orgone, bioenergy and others.*

As psychophysiological metaphor, fire *and flames are associated with ardor, sexual passion, anger, excitement, vitality, inspiration, vision, imagination, and intuition. All of these states and experiences are linked to the functions and structures of the neuro-endocrine systems, as well as the subtle energy-fields and the chakras.*

***Elemental Earth.** The* earth *elements at the planetary/ cosmic levels are the rocks, minerals, mountains, deserts, crystals, soil, vegetation, trees, roots — everything tangible with weight and substance. At the level of the human being this includes the living flesh and bones, muscles and other tissues, the skin, the hands and feet, and the sensory awareness associated with these structural organ* *and cell systems. Where* air *is associated with mind, water with feeling, fire with perception and intuition,* earth *is associated with sensation, sensitivity and sensuality — again everything tangible that can be weighed, held, and touched.* Earth *is the densest, heaviest, most solid of the four elemental states, what we ordinarily think of when say "matter." The alchemists say, "Elemental* earth *is like a sponge, and the receptacle of all the other elements."*

Integrating and Transmuting the Elements

The work of alchemy consisted of integrating and transmuting these elements, these levels of conscious-ness. They need to be integrated, because in the nor-mal condition of man they are in a state of conflict and confusion and are programmed by low-level images and imprints. The alchemists referred to this initial state as "chaos," or a "confused mass," or nigredo, "blackness." It was essential to recognize this state of inner chaos, the constant warfare of what Gurdjieff called the "many 'I's," before the work of transformation could begin.

Nigredo (Sp.) – "dense darkness". The dark place of depression, when everything seems dense, obscure and heavy. The "black mood," melancholia, when one feels stuck in obstacles and frustrations. Ordinary objects in the environment and other people appear visually dark, *as if covered in* dark *gauze, and look downcast, heavy as*

In the state of "chaos" the king (the higher nature) is lifeless, his body being devoured by predatory images (cf. Prometheus). But as the fire consumes the wolfish images, the king is liberated.

if carrying a burden — as indeed they are. There is no fixed rule about how long the nigredo as a depressed state of consciousness lasts — it could be days, months, or years, and it can also vary cyclically, as in manic-depressive disorders. It depends on how much intentional healing work you bring to bear on yourself. For the alchemist, this can be the starting point of the transformative process, when you seek help to get out of the black despair, either through psychotherapy, or through intentional inner-directed work. If left untreated the black depressed states can lead to suicide. Ernest Hemingway used the image of a black dog for his depressive, suicidal episodes.

"The elixir is composed by the reconciling and mutual transmutation of the four elements," says one alchemist.[20] Another text explains: "When corruptible elements are united in a certain subject, their strife must sooner or later bring about its decomposition . . . if the pure elements are then once more joined together by the action of natural heat, a much nobler and higher form of life is produced."[21] The integration of the bodies or levels of consciousness was often described by analogy with the chemical processes of "solution" and "coagulation": the former turns a solid into a liquid, the latter does the reverse. "The whole thing is done by a simple process of heating, which includes the solution and coagulation of bodies," writes the author of "The Only True Way."[22] "Dissolve and coagulate" became one of the oft-quoted maxims of the alchemists.

Solutio (L.) – dissolving. The process of reducing solids to fluids, as in melting and disintegrating a mix of two or more component solid substances. An image or dream vision can vanish and dissolve; a meeting of people on a project or a parliament can be dissolved*; a person may* dissolve *emotionally with tears in their eyes; an image in a photo or film may* dissolve *and change into another one. The traditional alchemical prescription –* solve et coagula *– "dissolve and coagulate" was saying: practice* dissolving *the rigid defensive patterns and coagulating or congealing new and healthier and fluid emotions into flexible patterns of thought and behavior.*

    A new alchemical prescription — dissolve and crystallize — is saying: dissolve *the old defensive emotion-thought defensive patterns and re-crystallize the purified energy essences, bringing more awareness and pure intention into the forms of mind and behavior. Gurdjieff talked about "premature crystallizations" that may have to be dissolved and re-formed again and again, since they may hold immature thought forms from an earlier time of your life, and are no longer appropriate.*

Coagulatio (L.) – *("curdling, congealing, coagulation"). This concept refers to the process by which a liquid is transformed into a soft, partially solid mass, becoming thicker and denser. Flowing river and heavy rain water* congeals *earth elements on a slope or hillside into muddy streams or torrents.*

Milk infused with small amounts of bacteria is partially or completely curdled into foods like yogurt and various cheeses, which can be preserved and stored much longer than fresh milk at room temperatures. Such curdled milk products have been parts of humanity's food treasures in all parts of the world since the most ancient times. The formation of partially coagulated *blood clots is an important aspect of natural healing in cases of bleeding wounds.*

Coagulation *in the human body applies at the cellular and the physiological organ level. In Wilhelm Reich's concept of the "muscular armoring," a military metaphor, there is congealing of cellular and tissue fluids. Muscle tissue becomes rigid and hard, reflecting emotional rigidity and defensiveness, and difficulty with relaxation. When the muscular armoring is dissolved, as can happen through directed breathing and bodywork, the individual becomes emotionally more present and relaxed, less armored and defensive.*

The integration of levels of consciousness was seen also as the spirit becoming body and the body becoming spiritualized. In "The Glory of the World" is a fascinating passage which unites many of these metaphors: "The gentle inward heat which changes it (the body) into water, and yields two waters, viz., the distilled spirit, and the dissolved body. These two waters are again united by slow and gentle concoction, the distilled spirit becoming coagulated into a body, the dissolved body becoming a spirit. The fixed becomes volatile, and the volatile fixed, by dissolution and coagulation."[23]

In one of the strange quirks of linguistic history the term distilled spirit, having lost its connection to the process of psychological transmutation, became the name for a type of chemically processed beverage prepared by the liquor industry; a beverage notable for its effect of blunting the spirit. The original alchemical "distillation of the spirit," was described as thousand fold and as circular, reminiscent of the "circulation of the light" of Chinese alchemy, and of the "thousand petal lotus" of the Hindu and Tibetan Tantras.

"Separation of the elements" was another frequently employed, and as frequently misunderstood, metaphor. Paracelsus wrote: "The impure animate body must be purified through the separation of the elements," and he goes on, "which is done by your meditating on it."[24]

In other words, it is clearly specified that the separation is in awareness. In the initial state of "confused mass," we are not aware of several bodies; our awareness gradually becomes more discriminating, and is able to separate the elements, that is, to distinguish the different levels of consciousness.

Some alchemists became very involved in describing the various inner changes that resulted from the work in chemical terms. As the image-factors obstructing clear consciousness are burned out by the inner fire, various processes analogous to "calcination," "putrefaction," "decomposition," "sublimation," etc., might indeed take place. Yet again some authors were dismayed by this trend toward multiple terminology, which they saw as a distraction from the basic simplicity of the method. In "The Only True Way," it is said the "substance" needs no special treatment, "except that of digestion by gentle heat. . . . For while you heat, you also putrefy, or decompose . . Again when you heat, you also sublime."[25] And indeed, this author is evidently quite correct in pointing out that the various chemical processes named are all the results and effects of heating. So that we may regard them as names for different stages of one process.

Calcinatio (L.) – *("calcination"). In the language of chemistry,* calcination *refers to the process of heating a material substance, such as chalk, to high temperature, but below the melting or fusing point. So* calcination *brings about loss of moisture, reduction or oxidation and a hardening of tissue.*

Since water and other fluids relate metaphorically to the wave-like up and down movements of the emotional nature, alchemical calcinatio *refers to psychophysical states or moods where that emotional fluidity is lost. If the hard dryness is carried to an extreme we may find the cold, unfeeling states of rigid, obsessive anger, and/or the hardhearted, with-holding attitude of such figures as the miserly old Scrooge, in Charles Dickens'* A Christmas Story.

The calcinatio *process can be part of a psychophysiological healing practice when it is self-chosen and self-controlled to support healing, as for example in the Finnish sauna, where physical and emotional impurities can be sweated out of the pores of skin.*

In the Native American group sweat lodge ceremony this practice explicitly includes the spiritual dimension, since the individuals sitting and sweating around an open fire in a closed tepee are guided by an experienced elder verbalizing teaching stories and prayers as the moist, watery bodies are sweating in the intense heat.

Sublimatio (L.) *– ("sublimating"). In chemistry to* sublimate *a substance is to transform it from a solid form to a gaseous state, without passing through a liquid state. In psychoanalysis to* sublimate *an impulse is to bring it into creative, not destructive, expression – a sexual attraction or desire may be* sublimated *into artistic expression in poetry, music or dance. An aggressive drive may be* sublimated *in a competitive sport like tennis or football. In the practice of alchemical yoga,* sublimatio *would involve the practice of raising the psychophysical energy-flow of atten-*

tion and expression from the centers in the lower abdo-men and pelvis to the centers in the heart-field, throat and head. Sublimation is also involved when the erotic drive is sublimated from the personal to the transpersonal and spiritual dimensions, as in the poetry and music of the Sufi mystics and medieval troubadours.

Sometimes, the purification or transmutation of ele-ments was described as a process of ascent, followed by descent. In the "Emerald Tablet" attributed to Hermes, it was said: "It ascendeth from the earth to heaven, and descendeth again to the earth, and receiveth the power of the higher and the lower things. So wilt thou have the glory of the whole world."[26] The ascent is of course not in a physical space, but rather in levels of consciousness, in frequency rate, through the four elements and higher states; and the descent is the return journey, which brings something of the quality of the higher levels into the lower. Thus, Gerhard Dorn, a seventeenth-century alchemist writes: "This earthly spagyric birth clothes itself with heavenly nature by its ascent, and then by its descent visibly puts on the nature of the centre of the earth, but nonetheless the nature of the heavenly centre which it acquired by the ascent is secretly preserved." This birth conquers the "subtle and spiritual sickness in the human mind and also all bodily defects, within as well as without."[27]

Purificatio (L.) – *("purification"). The core process of physical and psychic alchemy, a necessary preparation and* *accompaniment of all the other processes of transformation. The overlays, crusts and coverings over our patterns of perception, emotion and thought are like the rigidified muscles and bones on the physical level, the sticky swamps in the emotional nature or the foggy cobwebs in the attics of the mind. They need to be burned off with the fires of* purification *to permit the inherent pristine beauty, clarity, flexibility and radiance to become apparent.*

The Green Lion: Purificatio
The Green Lion Eats the Sun

At the level of individual yogic practice this aphorism refers to the practice of purificatio: *when you "eat" the Sun, you have fire in your belly; your psychometabolism is cooking in the abdominal cauldron.*

At the planetary level the "green lion" is a hybrid symbol of plant and animal life, "eats" means consumes and transforms, "Sun" means "solar energy". Modern science confirms the alchemists' insight: solar energy influx to planet Earth is harnessed by plants to build vegetative matter using chlorophyll, and then animals including humans eat these plants. So the statement is a condensed symbol of the basic biospheric ecosystem, which is sustained by solar energy through the symbiotic combination of plant and animal life.

The medical, healing properties of the "Stone," the goal of alchemy, are often emphasized: it was called "tincture," "panacea," "elixir of life," "spagyric medicine." Again, with the exception of certain of the physician specialists, it must not be supposed that the alchemists were preparing actual physical medicines. Rather, the transformation of self into a unified being in whom Immortal Self actualizes its highest potentials involves in part the ability to heal one's own earth-body, and to a certain degree the bodies of others. The great teachers have always been healers as well, not miracle healers or faith healers, but healers with higher energies.

As one might expect, the reputed or actual ability to heal sometimes got the alchemists into trouble from those who mistook the inner powers of the alchemists as being due to an external material. This was an additional reason for their secrecy, as is illustrated in the following story told by the author of "An Open Entrance": "It was only a short time ago that, after visiting the plague-stricken haunts of a certain city, and restoring the sick to health by means of my miraculous medicine, I found myself surrounded by a yelling mob, who demanded that I should give them my Elixir of the Sages; and it was only by changing my dress and my name, by shaving off my beard and putting on a wig, that I was able to save my life, and escape from the hands of those wicked men."[28] This is why the "fear closes our lips, when love tempts us to open ourselves freely to a brother." Mankind has ever tended to respond to the message of light with fear, greed, rage, envy, ingratitude, and destructive hate.

The alchemist-teachers required the highest qualities of character and devotion from their students because the difficulties of the work were such that without these qualities it could not be carried through, and because they were unwilling to have the techniques fall into the hands of those who would misuse them for their personal advantage.

By and large, the alchemists seem to have been extremely devout and sincere individuals. In their "Laboratory manuals" the phrase *Deo concedente*, "if God be willing," was appended to the descriptions of their experiments and their art. Though they knew that many of their doctrines, especially the emphasis on Nature as the revealer of truth, were anathema to established Christianity, which held that church and priest were the only guardians of truth, yet they saw themselves as followers of Christ, and as "God-fearing men." Carl Jung has devoted considerable research and scholarship to pointing out the many parallels between alchemy and early Christian mysticism, especially the Gnostic school and Manichaeism; and he has also suggested that the philosophers' Stone was in many ways synonymous with what the Christians called "the Christ," or "Christ-consciousness," or "the body of Christ."

The following passage, from the treatise entitled "The Sophic Hydrolith," is typical of the alchemists' attitude:

> In the first place, let every devout and God-fearing chemist and student of the Art consider that this Arcanum should be regarded, not only as a truly great, but as a most holy Art (seeing that it typifies and shadows out the highest heavenly good). Therefore, if any

man desire to reach this great and unspeak-
able Mystery, he must remember that it is
obtained not by the might of man, but by
the grace of God, and that not our will or
desire, but only the Mercy of the Most High
can bestow it upon us. . . When you have
thus devoted yourself to God and learned to
appreciate justly the aim and scope of this
Art, you should, in the first place, strive to
realize how Nature, having been set in order
by God the Triune, now works invisibly day
by day, and moves and dwells in the will of
God alone. For no one should set about the
study of this Art without a just appreciation
of the natural processes. Now Nature may
truly be described as being one, true, simple,
and perfect in her own essence, and as being
animated by an invisible spirit. If therefore
you would know her, you, too, should be
true single-hearted, patient, constant, pious,
forbearing, and, in short, a new and regenerate man.[29]

The counsel of patience is ubiquitous in the alchemical literature. They warned that undue haste could
be destructive to the work, an explosion could wreck
the "furnace" and wipe out many months of effort. By
explosions the alchemists presumably meant explosions
of anger, or rage, which, if let out, could upset the del-
icate balancing of internal chemistry, which the art was

trying to bring about. Gurdjieff used to say one moment of anger cost him three pints of blood.

Besides haste, the other main obstacle the alchemists warned of was despair or discouragement. As an antidote to this, "The Ordinal of Alchemy" counsels that "you should take care, from time to time, to unbend your mind from its sterner employments with some convenient recreation; otherwise, your spirits might be weighed down with melancholy and despair, and you might lose heart for the continuation of the work."[30]

The Three Forces

We have seen how the principle of integrating four aspects of the nature of man is of central importance in alchemy. Most often the four are designated earth, water, air and fire. Sometimes the process is said to be one of the correct adjustments of the four qualities dry, moist, hot, and cold, which were related to the four humors, or psycho-physiological dispositions to be sanguine, melancholic, choleric, or phlegmatic. The common-sense psychology of everyday speech still recognizes these four types, even though rational minds consider them outmoded: we all know the "dry humor" of the sanguine character, the melancholic's "dampening" effect on our spirits, the "hot temper" of the choleric, and the "cool" of the phlegmatic.

Besides the principle of four, the quaternary, the alchemists also attached great importance to the trinity, the duality and the singularity. In the treatise "The New Chemical Light," by Michael Sendivogius, the three principles "sulphur," "salt," and "mercury" are said to arise from the interaction of the four elements. And then, "as the three principles are produced out of four, so they, in turn, must produce two, a male and a female; and these two must produce an incorruptible one, in which are exhibited the four elements in a highly purified and digested condition, and with their mutual strife hushed in unending peace and goodwill."[31]

In other words, the work is here described as beginning with the mutual balancing and harmonizing of the four bodies or levels of consciousness, from which arises an awareness of the three primary forces, and when these are polarized as male and female (Sun and Moon, king and queen), they can be united in the chemical wedding, and from this conjunction will come the philosophers' Stone, the "elixir of the Sages."

The trinity sulphur, salt, and mercury, at least in the later alchemical writings, is conceived as a trio of forces interacting in everything. "That universal thing, the greatest treasure of earthly wisdom, is one thing, and the principles of three things are found in one . . . The three things are the true spirit of mercury, and the soul of sulphur, united to a spiritual salt, and dwelling in one body."[32] This is comparable to the yang, yin, and Tao of Chinese philosophy, and the Hindu trinity of Brahma, Siva, and Vishnu. We recall also Gurdjieff's formulation of the Law of Three: that everything is a product of the interaction of affirming, denying, and reconciling forces. For the alchemists, sulphur is the active, dynamic principle; salt is the female, magnetic; and mercury or quicksilver is double-natured, ubiquitous and fluid, like the water of the Taoists. (It must be said though that in some texts only two forces are described, in which case sulphur is active and mercury passive.)

Sulphur is related to Sun, the male aspect in the conjunction. According to Gerhard Dorn, "The male and universal seed, the first and most potent, is the solar sulphur, the first part and the most potent cause of generation."[33] It is also referred to as "the homogeneous sperm," as "living fire," which "quickens and matures lifeless substances," and as "the spirit of generative power, who works in the moisture." In its crude untransmuted form, sulphur, if excessive, is the "cause of corruption," it is of an "evil, stinking odor and not much strength;" but, transmuted, it becomes, "the virtue of all things," and is compared to a rainbow.

The change undergone by sulphur, the male principle, in the course of the work, is indicated in "An Open Entrance," where it is said that "the coagulating sulphur, which in the corporal god was turned outwards, is turned inwards;"[34] this inward turning comes about when the Sun and Moon are united. In other words, inner unity is brought about by the male principle seeking its own female consort *within* nature, rather than externally.

Salt, because of its association with the sea and hence the Moon, was seen as a feminine, lunar principle. It is referred to as the "permanent radical moisture," as the "concentrated centre of the elements," as "common

Moon," and as the "white water." In its initial, impure state, it is "bitter" and "harsh," also "black and evil-smelling." Transmuted, it is called *albedo*, "whiteness." It is the tincture that coagulates all substances, even itself. "The salt alkali is hidden in the womb of magnesia," says "The New Chemical Light."[35] And in "The Golden Tract" it is said that "he who works without salt will never raise dead bodies . . . he who works without salt draws a bow without a string."[36] Thus, salt is the structural, feminine, magnetic principle; also salt is the wisdom principle. "And the Light was made Salt, a body of salt, the salt of wisdom,"[37] according to the alchemist Khunrath.

The association of salt with wisdom is ancient, and is found in the Gospels, where Jesus refers to his disciples as the "salt of the earth," and admonishes them to "have salt in yourselves." The colloquial expression "with a grain of salt," still carries this meaning. Wisdom, as an aspect of the feminine half of the nature, is embodied by Egyptian mythology in the figure of Isis (the High Priestess of the Tarot), by Greek myth in the figure of Athena, and by American myth in the concept of *alma mater*, literally "nourishing mother." The preservative qualities of common salt may have contributed to its choice as the metaphor for the sustaining mother-principle.

Just as the attempt to define *Tao* led Laotse into his most mind-baffling paradoxical statements, so the attempt to describe the nature of *mercurius* caused the alchemists to produce some of their most fantastic formulations. Here for example is a passage from "the Chemical Light," in which Nature, in response to a question from the Alchemist, describes *Mercury*, her son: "Know that I have only one such son; he is one of seven, and the first among them; and though he is now all things, he was at first only one. In him are the four elements, yet he is not an element. He is a spirit, yet he has a body; a man, yet he performs a woman's part; a boy, yet he bears a man's weapons; a beast, yet he has wings of a bird. He is poison, yet he cures leprosy; life, yet he kills all things; a King, yet another occupies his throne; he flees from the fire, yet fire is taken from him; he is water, yet does not wet the hands; he is earth, yet is sown; he is air, and lives by water."[38]

In a German version of the well-known tale of the genie in the bottle, the name of the imprisoned spirit is Mercurius. A little boy finds a bottle (the "hermetic vessel") in the forest, and a spirit within, calling to be let out. When he lets him out, Mercurius grows to the size of a giant tree. Later, as a reward, Mercurius gives the boy something that both heals and turns metals into silver.

Silver – *(argentum nostrum (L.), "our silver"). Silver, the precious metal, has numerous uses in society — as coinage and store of value, as a medium for artistic expression in jewelry and personal wear. Because it can be tarnished and also exists in greater abundance,* silver *the metal is considered less valuable than gold in commerce and coinage. In alchemical yoga,* silver *light-fire energy is associated with the cosmic mother archetype. It is visualized in the form of a* silver *chalice located about 6" above the crown of the head, from where the fluid* silvery *energy can pour down throughout and around the entire body and energy-field. The silver energy as an experience is described as having a nurturing, healing and comforting quality. It can also be experienced as fierce maternal protection – as is well known that a mother mammal is the most dangerous animal to anyone threatening to harm its offspring. In the alchemical yoga practice, the offspring would be the mind-body persona of the practitioner.*

We would say Mercury is consciousness; consciousness exists on many different levels (elements), can assume many guises, be male or female, young or old, bird or beast; normally, it is restricted, "bottled up," though it has the potential of a giant, of a tree. The mobile elusive fluidity of quicksilver make it an apt choice of metaphor for consciousness.

Mercury is described as "dry water," as "root moisture," as "invisible fire," and "scintillating fire of the light of nature"; as "stone uplifted by the wind" and as "winged and wingless dragon."[39] Even more graphic is his characterization as the dragon Pantophthalmos, who is covered with eyes all over his body, and sleeps with some open and some closed. He is also called "duplex," "inconstant," "changing his skin," a "hermaphroditic monster," "good with the good and evil with the evil." These designations are suggestive of the image-producing power of consciousness, the polymorphous perversity of ever changing, shape-shifting images with which consciousness is programmed. Mercury is everywhere, goes everywhere, to the highest and the lowest, the lightest and the heaviest, earth and heavy, strong and weak;

he is akin to the God-head, yet he is found in sewers. He is referred to as *terminus ani,* "end of the anus," but also as "carbuncle of the Sun."

Mercury's role as mediator between sulphur and salt, between male and female, between spirit and body, is clearly indicated when he is called *anima media natura,* "soul of intermediate nature" or "intermediate substance." Probably the most concise summary of his nature and role is "Mercurius is the medium of the conjunction."[40] Inner unification takes place in the medium, the neutral field of consciousness. "living mercury . . . promotes fusion . . . it is full of affinity, cleaving faithfully, and is the medium by which tinctures are united, for it mingles most intimately with them, penetrating into their inmost part, for it is of the same nature."[41]

The four, the three, the two, and the one.
(Squaring the circle.)

The Two Opposites

The "union of opposites" in alchemy is most often described as the "conjunction of Sun and Moon," also called "gold" and "silver." "Gold, then, being the most precious of all the metals, is the red tincture, tinging and transforming everybody. Silver is the white tincture, tinging other bodies with its perfect whiteness."[42] The text goes on to explain that gold and silver are not meant here in their metallic form; no other tincture is meant "but our own." "There is no acid but our own, no other regimen, no other colors." Sun is described as a "living fire," "ruddy and burning." The philosophers' gold is a "quickening ferment" which must be sown into the "earth." Alternatively, the "living gold" must be extracted from its "ore," which is the "earth." It is called "regenerate gold," whose red color is due to the admixture of copper. In the alchemical drawings, the Sun is usually shown above and to the right of the adept, or sometimes he is standing upon it. The Moon is above and to the left, or, sometimes, the female has the Moon below her feet.

"Gold," or "Sun," or "red tincture" would seem to be names for an aspect of inner work: a tool of transmutation, of purification, and transformation. The transmutation takes place in consciousness, at least to begin with, and is brought about through the action of fire. Mercury multiplies gold, but "in virtue, rather than in weight."[43] In other words, consciousness amplifies the transformative power.

The alchemical masculine and feminine aspects of nature, mixing chemicals in the vessel (within) until finally the Sun, the power of transmutation, bearing the golden flower, appears.

Gold – *(aurum nostrum (L.), "our gold"). Gold, as a precious metal, is traditionally used for coinage and regarded as a medium for the store of value, as well as being crafted for artistic expression in jewelry and ornamentation. The alchemists associated* gold *with the cosmic father principle,* *and visualized its microcosmic source as a* golden *dome-shaped crown on the chakra above the top of the head. This dome-shaped crown can be seen portrayed in various paintings and sculptures in both Western religious and Buddhist iconography. In the practice of alchemical yoga, the energy from the* golden *crown pours, liquid-like, down and throughout the head and entire body. It has a protective quality and can generally transform negative and depressing energy in the mind-body persona into a positive, protective and uplifting aura.*

"Moon" in alchemy is the source of moisture, of "hidden dew," also of "appetites" and emotions such as anger and desire. It is said that "the realm of the perishable begins with the Moon,"[44] and the Moon is said to be the "contriver of bodie." "Hence the body, or Moon, has been well-designated the female principle, and the water, or Sun, the male principle."[45] Lunar mythology is associated with animals such as dragons, serpents, scorpions, toads; lions bears wolves, dogs; eagles and ravens. Reptiles, mammals and birds appear in awareness, in approximately this order, as a result of the conjunction of Sun and Moon. The "Moon" is regarded as the preserver of past evolutionary tendencies and imprints. If these animal, lunar, consciousness factors usurp the human level of consciousness, "lunacy" results. But when the transformative power of the "red-gold Sun" is brought to bear upon them, these animal forms will appear in consciousness and be transmuted.

The alchemists were much concerned with the animal aspects of our nature, or what in Actualism would be called the creature-body level of consciousness, which has powerful residual imprints and images left over from past evolutionary stages. One alchemical drawing shows a wolf and a dog fighting with fury and jealous rage. (The wolf and dog appear also in the Moon card of the Tarot.) This is the struggle between the wild and the domesticated animal nature, fighting the evolutionary battle for survival. Hermann Hesse wrote of this conflict in *Steppenwolf.* Fritz Perls called it the struggles between "top dog" and "under dog." For the alchemists, when these two are changed into one, they become "the most great and precious medicine." The transmutation of animal, lunar consciousness is also indicated in the frequent verbal and visual references to crowned serpents, crowned birds, or winged mammals, or mammals with human heads.

"A wolf and a dog are in one house, and are afterwards changed into one."

"Hear without terror that in the forest are hidden a deer and a unicorn. In the body there is soul and spirit."

The conjunction of male and female creature body levels of consciousness. "Here you behold a great marvel – two lions are joined into one."

The conjunction of opposites was described in many different ways under different aspects. One might say the union has to take place on all levels of consciousness. On the level of the animal, creature body, we find representations of the lion and the lioness. The marriage of king and queen is the union of transmuted male and female energies. The English alchemist John Prodage described it as the union of Mars, "the fiery life," and Venus, "the gentle love-fire."[46] It was also seen as the marriage of spirit and body, the integration of the highest and the lowest, that is, high-frequency and low-frequency levels of consciousness, fire and water. In the words of Avicenna, "Marriage is the mingling of the subtle with the dense."[47]

In a series of drawings illustrating stages of the conjunction, the *hieros gamos* or "sacred marriage," one can see how the alchemists conceived the gradual, progressive unification of the male and female within.[48] At first, there is a man on the left with a Sun beneath his feet, and a woman on the right with the Moon beneath her feet. They are giving each other their left hands, and with their right hands are holding crossed branches. Centered above is a star, and a dove is descending, holding another branch. At first, awkward, "gauche" contact has been made between the two halves of the nature, with the help of the bird of peace and the light of the star.

In the next picture, the couple is naked; they confront each other more openly, undisguised and undefensive. Each one is holding the branch from the opposite hand of the other, indicating greater interrelatedness. Sol, the male, solar force, says: "O Luna, let me be your husband." Luna, the female, lunar force, says: "O Sol, I will be receptive to you."

In the following picture, the man and woman are immersed in the bath. They are being bathed, purified, heated; impurities, factors obstructing the union, are being dissolved out. "Our Stone is to be extracted from the nature of the two bodies," says the accompanying text.

In the next picture, solar king and lunar queen are mating. They are under the earth and in the water: the conjunction takes place in the "earth-body" and in the emotional "waters of life." The pictorial version of this stage shows them each with a pair of wings, indicating even more clearly the multidimensional nature of this conjunction: in earth, in water, and in air. Sol says: "O Luna, through my embrace and sweet love, you become beautiful and strong as I am." Luna says "O Sol, though your light is the brightest, yet you need me as the cock the hen." The text says, "In the hour of conjunction the greatest marvels appear." And "The new light is begotten by them."

In the following picture, king and queen have fused into a single being with two heads. They are shown in a tomb, because the old has died, and the new is yet to be born. "The death of one is the generation of the other." This is the classic theme of regeneration through death and rebirth. This is by no means the end of the process: in subsequent pictures the soul is shown ascending, leaving the body, the body is further purified, by dew from above, and the soul returns into the new, lighted, unified, androgynous body. This being was called "son" or "daughter" of the philosophers. "Now is the Stone shaped, the elixir of life prepared, the love-child or the child of love born, the new birth completed, and the work made whole and perfect." [49]

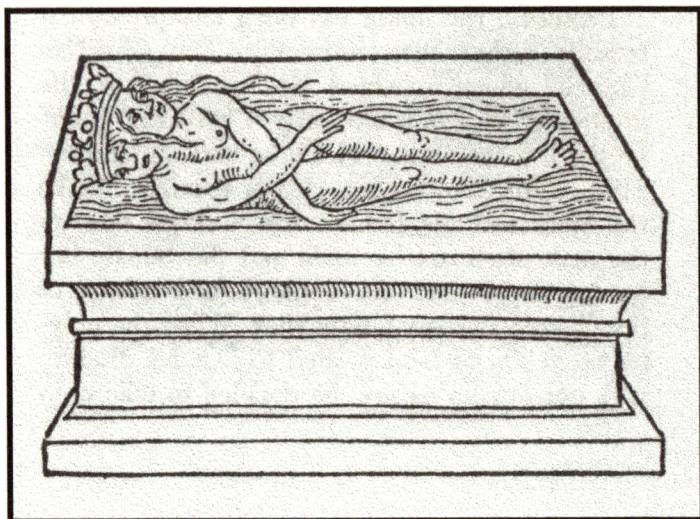

No aspect of the teaching of alchemy, or of esoteric philosophy in general, has been as misunderstood as the concept of the conjunction or royal marriage. The difficulty of communication stems from the fact that we are dealing with an experience, and a rare one. To one who has not had the experience, or anything like it, the words are sheer fantasy. In addition, the alchemists themselves were most allegorical and reticent about this aspect of their work. In the *Rosarium Philosophorum,* it was said: "So I have not declared all that appears and is necessary in this work, because there are things of which a man may not speak." And: "Such matters must be transmitted in mystical terms, like employing fables and parables."[50]

There is another reason why it is so difficult to communicate and understand this process of inner union of male and female. There are very strong psychic image-factors and imprints which prevent us from coming to a just appreciation of this most vital secret. There are internal defense screens which block us from perceiving and experiencing this union. It is precisely for this reason that the art has been so difficult: all kinds of false interpretations of the meaning of this marriage are superimposed on the actual meaning, which Higher Self knows.

Typically, the union has been interpreted externally rather than internally. The Christian Church, which received the teaching of the mystic union from the early Christians, interpreted it as the union of Christ and the church. Thus, Christ had taught, clearly enough: "Make the male and the female into a single one, so the male shall not be male and the female not be female."[51] Yet, St. Gregory and others of the Church Fathers taught that "When the only-begotten son of God wished to join his divinity with our human nature, he decided to take unto himself, as his bride, the Church."[52] The union is no longer inner, but outer.

Jung himself, in spite of his lengthy and profound study of the alchemical texts and his high sensitivity and intuition, did not really grasp this point. In his book *Psychology of the Transference* he interprets the conjunction in terms of the transference relationship between doctor and patient; again, an external union rather than the inner.

Freud's theory of the "primal scene" is another image-distortion of the actual inner union. Freud held that most children at some time see their parents copulating and this implants a traumatic, fearful image of sexual union. From the esoteric or alchemical point of view, we can see the whole notion of the traumatic primal scene taking place "out there" as a defensive fantasy screen, preventing awareness of the potential creative union of the divine Father and Mother within. For, as the *Rosarium* says: "When my beloved parents have tasted of life, . . . and have embraced each other in my bed, they shall bring forth the son of the Moon, who will excel all his kindred."[53] Or, in the words of Paracelsus: "When the heavenly marriage is accomplished, who will deny its superexcellent virtue?"[54]

The One Stone

When the offspring of the inner union has been tested, purified, tempered, and strengthened by repeated ascents and descents, by distillation and sublimation, the long sought-after philosophers' Stone is produced, "the most ancient, sacred, natural, incomprehensible, heavenly, blessed, beatified, and triune universal Stone of the Sages."[55] "This child of the two parents, of the elements and heaven, has in itself such a nature that the potentiality and the actuality of both parents can be found in it. What will remain there til today, save the Stone in the spagyric generation?"[56] But what is this Stone? "It is called perfect because it has in itself the nature of mineral, vegetable and animal. For the Stone is triple and one, having four natures."[57] "It is called a Stone, not because it is like a stone, but only because, by virtue of its fixed nature, it resists the action of fire."[58] According to the "Emerald Tablet" attributed to Hermes, "The Sun is its Father, the Moon its Mother, the wind bears it in its womb, and it is nursed by the earth."[59] Thus the Stone would seem to be a power, or ability, which is acquired in the alchemical art, through conjunction of Sun and Moon; this power grows at first in the air element, the mental level of consciousness; it is nourished and strengthened in the earth element, the physical body. It is called the "flower of gold," i.e., it is the product (flower) of the transmutation process (gold).

And where is the Stone to be found? "Our Stone is found in all the mountains, all trees, all herbs, and animals and with all men. It wears many different colors, contains the four elements, and has been designated a microcosm."[60] It is ubiquitous; it enters into everything. It involves a synthesis of elements, of bodies, or levels of consciousness. "This Stone is under you, and near you, and above you, and around you."[61] But mostly, it is within you: "This thing is extracted from you, for you are its ore; . . . and when you have experienced this, the love and desire for it will be increased in you."[62]

Russell Schofield, the founder of Actualism, said that "The philosophers' Stone is not a magical object; it is the magnificent condition resulting from reaching the objective."[63] The Stone is the ability to be objective about fact, to perceive and know the "hard" fact of a given situation as it actually is, without preconceived ideas and images distorting the fact. Hence, the Stone was said to be one, though it could be infinitely multiplied: a fact is unitary, immutable; yet the ability to know the fact, once it has been acquired, can be infinitely extended to all situations--all mountains, all herbs, etc. It was also said that the Stone is water: to know the fact from all aspects one must maintain fluidity of perspective. "Standing firmly on a moving point" is an Actualist phrase for this perceptual mobility.

To know objectively is to know with the certainty that one knows. It is to know the essence of the fact from all levels of consciousness, all four elements; hence the Stone was called the "fifth essence," the quintessence or perfect manifestation. The alchemist Geber said: "It illumines all bodies, since it is the light of the light, and their tincture."[64] This Stone, this "father of miracles," is acquired through a process analogous to mining: the "bedrock" of truth has to be separated from the ore. The superimposed distortions have to be dissolved, until only that which cannot be dissolved remains: the "rock-bottom," the "Stone."

One may ask why the alchemical adepts went to such extraordinary lengths to conceal in metaphor and parable something as straightforward as the ability to be objective. Why not just say it the way it is? Because to do so would be to invite misunderstanding. "Our substance is openly displayed before the eyes of all, and yet is not known."[65] "Learned doctors . . . have it before their eyes every day, but they do not understand it, because they never attend to it."[66] It is misunderstood primarily because people do not realize that the work of finding the Stone has first and foremost to be performed within. "We cannot be resolved of any doubt save by experiment, and there is no better way to make it than on ourselves," wrote Dorn.[67] Both the obstructions to truth and truth itself lie within us.

We cannot be objective about anything external until we can be objective about ourselves. To be objective means to be whole. "The goal of our art is not reached until Sun and Moon are conjoined, and become, as it were, one body."[68] This body is a kin to the "diamond body" of the Buddhist Tantras, the "immutable wisdom" of the "adamantine essence." It is indeed a totally transmuted body, a whole, illumined, multidimensional, objective consciousness. "When the pure and essential elements are joined together in loving equilibrium, as they are in our Stone, they are inseparable and immortal like the human body in Paradise."[69]

The New Alchemy

The wisdom of the alchemists was very ancient and timeless. It was, in essence, the same teaching that has arisen at other times and places: the wisdom of wholeness and how to attain it. Their metaphors and symbols were suggested by the concepts of the science of their day. In this new age, a new alchemy will undoubtedly arise that will take into account everything the chemists have learned, and will provide more comprehensive and satisfying formulations.

This will come about when individuals among the

natural scientists awake to the simple yet momentous fact that everything that can be studied "out there" can also, and better, be studied "in here." For the barriers to scientific objectivity lie within; the doubts have to be resolved by inner experiments, and the evolutionary purpose can only be understood and accomplished within. Afterwards it can also be externalized. If it be asked how I can be so sure of this, I will answer, like the alchemists, that I know it by experiment and experience.

Gurdjieff attempted to formulate a revised alchemy. In his "table of hydrogens" described in Ouspensky's *In Search of the Miraculous,* he set up a scale of "matters" of different densities or frequency rates, from the highest to the lowest. A segment of this spectrum was the range of matters that involved man. "The chemistry of which we speak here studies matter on a different basis from ordinary chemistry and takes into consideration not only the chemical and physical, but also the psychic and cosmic properties of matter."[70]

A new alchemy is particularly necessary for the true understanding of psychedelic substances, which are substances whose cosmic and psychic properties are startlingly evident. These substances were not unknown to the old alchemists. Paracelsus in particular makes many allusions to herbs and drugs. Cheyri (the yellow wallflower, *Cheiranthus cheiri*) "fortifies the microcosmic body . . . so that it must be necessary to continue in its conservation through the universal anatomy of the four elements."[71] Thereniabin, or oil of manna (*pinguedo manna*), also known as honeydew, was said to be "heavenly food," and "assist sublimination."[72] It has been suggested that since honeydew is the secretion of certain kinds of fungus, particularly the ergot fungus *claviceps purpurea*, which contains alkaloids of the LSD family, it is not impossible that this "manna" had psychedelic properties.[73] Other "arcane remedies" mentioned by Paracelsus include Nostoch, a gelatinous algae, also known as "star jelly" or "witches' butter"; and (*melissa officinalis*), a "balm" that was said to have the power of "supracelestial conjunction." These four are called *anaiada*, and are said to produce "exaltation in both worlds," and to promote longevity.

From a chemical point of view it has often been proposed that psychedelic substances act like catalysts in the nervous system; that is, they facilitate a chemical change in the fluids surrounding nerve cells so that these cells will respond with increased rate of flow of electrical impulses. The heightened perceptual sensitivity is equivalent to a reduced firing threshold of neurons. This increased responsiveness could lead to a temporary release from neurophysiologic imprints. As one alchemist said: "The drug being ignited, the shadow of the dense body is to be stripped away."[74]

Most catalysts are reversible, and they will equally well facilitate the reaction from A to B as the one from B to A. This appears to be true of LSD. If the prevailing current, metaphorically speaking, is to clear existing programs, it will facilitate this clearing. If on the other hand, the consciousness field is dominated by mental or emotional imprints, these will be magnified. Psychedelics

can heighten clarity of perception and flow of awareness; or they can still further intensify the muddiness of
clouded viewpoints and amplify negative feelings. They
can "cleanse the doors of perception" or obscure them
still further. This is why LSD is only a tool for amplifi-
cation. It is not *by itself* a reliable guide to direction or
purpose or means of attaining wholeness.

The psychedelic drugs have proved for many people to be powerful awakeners to the possibilities of consciousness to the Promethean potentials that are chained,
immobilized, and unactualized in most of us. Thus, the
discovery and synthesis of psychedelics is in the true
alchemical tradition of studying Nature to find aids for
man's evolutionary growth. Among physicians, the Natu-
ropaths and Homeopaths who use natural remedies and
endeavor to strengthen the body's own innate regenerative powers are the inheritors of the alchemical tradition.
The extraordinary potency of LSD, which far exceeds that
of any other known drug, suggests that the mechanism of
its action may be similar to what the Homeopaths refer
to as their "dynamized serial solutions."[75]

In the new alchemy, current knowledge of biochem-
istry and psychopharmacology would be integrated into
an experimentally verifiable understanding of the psychophysiological energy systems, rather than being, as
now, a mass of separate, unsynthesized data. It will now
be found, as it was found by the old alchemists, that there
are certain laws that are operative at every level of energy
organization and corresponding level of consciousness.

The modern theory of acid-base regulation in the

bloodstream is not unrelated to the alchemists' conception of sulphur and salt. Acids carry a positive charge in aqueous solutions, bases a negative charge. "Acid and base in solution react to form a salt" by a process of "neutralization."[76] By maintaining the hydrogen ion concentration of the blood, the balance of acid and base has an important effect on the psyche. It is known that excessive positive ionization of the atmosphere, as found today in our polluted cities, reduces the energy charge of the total organism, whereas a predominance of negative ions, as found in the country, increases the charge-carrying capacity of the organism and produces a feeling of vitality and buoyancy. Acid-base regulation is the "conjunction" of positive and negative energies on the molecular level.

The old alchemists frequently referred to the need for "digestion" by "gentle cooking" with "living fire." We are dealing here with what Sir Julian Huxley called "psychometabolism": the processing of experience-information by the brain and nervous system paralleling the processing of food by the digestive system. Experiences that are not digested, that "can't be stomached," leave residues obstructing the free flow of energy. On the emotional level we recognize these residues as "traumatic complexes." On the physiological and nervous level they are experienced as "crystallizations." In body-work of the Rolfian or Reichian type, these crystallizations can be literally felt, producing sharp pain when probed.

Crystallization. This is the process that transforms a vapor or a liquid to a solid. Drops of water vapor in the extreme cold of the upper atmosphere become ice crystals or snow flakes as they descend towards the earth's surface. As they descend even closer to the ground, they can melt or thaw into water as rain.

Crystals *are atoms or molecules arranged in regular, periodically repeated symmetrical lattices. Sand consists of silicates with an irregular, amorphous, asymmetrical structure. Sand can be transformed into glass through fire. Psychological* crystallization, *as in the arts, requires the heat of the fire of attention, just as the increasing heat of closeness to earth transforms the snow into rain.*

In the context of human consciousness and creativity we may think of crystallization *as the transformation of a mixed set of beliefs, thoughts, and emotions into a story or poem or invention that expresses the essential core.*

Thought-forms are crystallized *conceptions — crystallizations of akashic or etheric molecules that carry meaning. A thought that says "I'm afraid" or "I'm going to hurt you" are thought-forms crystallized from fear or hatred analogous to "hate mail".*

In the arts, a vision may be received in a dream or moment of inspiration and is then crystallized by the artist into a structure – verbal or visual or poetic or musical.

***

Coagulation and crystallization *are both transformations of a liquid becoming solid, "water into earth", but coagulation or clotting applies at room temperature, as in the formation of yogurt or cheese, and* crystallization *requires*

The transmutation of animal aspects of the nature by "gentle cooking" in the hermetic vessel. Note the **lingam-yoni** *symbol on the vessel.*

higher temperatures to first purify the liquid. The traditional motto dissolve and coagulate applies at the level of mixed cellular tissue, like blood and milk at room temperature.

Dissolve and crystallize *was not identified in traditional alchemy because it applies at the molecular level, in purified substances.* Crystallization *can only occur in purified substances, and so needs purification to precede it.*

Much harder to reach are the imprint structures and image-factors, which through long-term hereditary and cultural conditioning processes, have become crystallized in the brain. It is part of the art of alchemy to dissolve these *crystallizations* so that consciousness can function unobstructedly, so that higher frequency energy systems can appear more solidly in awareness. "Dissolve and coagulate" are alchemical processes in service of expanded consciousness.

Again and again the alchemists returned to their theme of studying the "possibilities of Nature," and following Nature in her simplicity, of making experiments in order to resolve any doubts. They counseled that books should be studied, but only to a limited degree, for they can lead astray, whereas Nature does not. So "rend the books lest your hearts be rent asunder."[77] Alchemy is not armchair philosophy or speculative science. It is the practice of inner union on all levels of consciousness, separately and conjoined. "Many strive to accomplish this separation and conjunction; but few succeed in bringing about a union which can stand the test of fire."[78]

Experiential Experiments

The methods of the alchemical adept of course cannot be described. However, it is possible to develop a sensory-physical understanding of their ideas. By reading, the mind can only know about something. True understanding however involves "standing," the earth-body and the cells must know it by experiencing it.

We can try to get a sense of what the elements are within us. What is the aspect of our consciousness that feels earthy, solid? Can we feel those structural elements throughout? Can we let ourselves sink into earth like into a receptacle?

And water — can we let ourselves dissolve into the fluid medium of life? Can we feel the liquid motion of emotion, as it washes through us? Can we distinguish the sharp spurting of adrenaline in the motions of fear and rage; and the slow, expansive melting of soothing joy; the salty bitterness of waves of grief; and the balmy sweetness of pleasure?

It is worth trying to experience the mixing of these aspects of consciousness: fluid feeling becoming volatile thought; fiery energy sinking into earth structures; an idea condensing into a feeling, or subliming into a tangible solid, like a snow crystal. "Make the fixed volatile, and the volatile fixed."

An experiment can be set up analogous to the one described: an external fire, or candle, is lit. Here it is best to use whatever form of meditation the person has found most efficacious. Let that internal focal point link up with the sound or visual aspect of the outer fire. The "I" becomes an observer or witness.

It is fruitful also to observe the differences, if any, between the left and right side of the body. The alchemical androgynous consciousness, as his tantric counterpart, is polarized dynamic male on the right and magnetic female on the left. By observing the differences in body sensation in the two halves of the earth-body, we can learn about attitudes, feelings, and images that the two halves of our nature have toward each other. And we can also begin to see how these attitudes, feelings, and images are projected out onto external individuals in male or female form.

One minute of such experimental self-observation is worth several hours of reading. And that's true.

Part Two
ALCHEMICAL
TERMS

Absorption

In the physical sciences we say a fluid is absorbed into a material solid when it is wholly taken and retained without reflection or transmission. As a metaphor in psychophysical alchemy this operation signifies that our emotional attention and interest (water) is more or less completely taken in by some activity or situation (earth) as water may be more or less completely absorbed into earth. Thus *absorption* signifies an operation that is related to alchemical water, i.e. the emotional nature.

When we are *absorbed* in something — a person, an activity, reading, performing a chosen task, or practicing an art, our attention and emotional interest are more or less completely involved, without distraction. Just as *absorption* of a fluid into a solid may be complete or partial, our interest and attention may be completely or intermittently focused in some activity or perception. Note that the name of the operation itself is morally neutral and does not imply a judgment or approval — e.g. a criminal safebreaker may be completely absorbed in his chosen task.

Psychological *absorption* can also be recognized as potentially a stage in an addictive process — an *absorbing* interest can lead, under predisposing conditions, to more or less complete addiction, such as in alcoholism, or compulsive gambling.

Albedo ("clear, white", L. *albus*)

In the scientific and everyday language of optics, *albedo* is defined as "the fraction of incident electromagnetic radiation is reflected by a surface." In other words, it is the reflected whiteness of a white sheet of paper, or a white painted wall, or a white dress, or a relatively white or light skin color. (The idea of a "white race" is an erroneous conflation of relative lightness of skin color with emotionally charged prejudices of racial superiority.)

On the level of life-cycle development, the symbolic image of the white-haired old man or woman *(senex albus, seneca alba)* refers to the archetype of the wise elder man or woman, who embodies and expresses the wisdom of accumulated experience. It should be understood that the archetype of the white-haired old man or woman is an image of *potential* wise elderhood that does not automatically correlate with simply being a man or woman old in number of years lived.

On the level of experiential alchemy, *albedo* as psychic inner radiance may appear as a phase of the alchemical *opus*. These phases do not occur in an invariant sequence. Rather our mood or psychic attitude can and does cycle back and forth repeatedly, over periods of days or months or even years, between a dark, depressed, *nigredo* blackness, a fiery, passionate *rubedo* redness, and a calm, light-hearted *albedo* whiteness.

Calcinatio (L.) ("calcination")

In the language of chemistry, *calcination* refers to the process of heating a material substance, such as chalk, to high temperature, but below the melting or fusing point. So *calcination* brings about loss of moisture, reduction or oxidation and a hardening of tissue.

Since water and other fluids relate metaphorically to the wave-like up and down movements of the emotional nature, alchemical *calcinatio* refers to psychophysical states or moods where that emotional fluidity is lost. If the hard dryness is carried to an extreme we may find the cold, unfeeling states of rigid, obsessive anger, and/or the hard-hearted, withholding attitude of such figures as the miserly old Scrooge, in Charles Dickens' *A Christmas Story.*

The *calcinatio* process can be part of a psychophysiological healing practice when it is self-chosen and self-controlled to support healing, as for example in the Finnish sauna, where physical and emotional impurities can be sweated out of the pores of skin.

In the Native American group sweat lodge ceremony this practice explicitly includes the spiritual dimension, since the individuals sitting and sweating around an open fire in a closed tepee are guided by an experienced elder verbalizing teaching stories and prayers as the moist, watery bodies are sweating in the intense heat.

Coagulatio (L.)

("curdling, congealing, coagulation")

This concept refers to the process by which a liquid is transformed into a soft, partially solid mass, becoming thicker and denser. Flowing river and heavy rain water *congeals* earth elements on a slope or hillside into muddy streams or torrents.

Milk infused with small amounts of bacteria is partially or completely curdled into foods like yogurt and various cheeses, which can be preserved and stored much longer than fresh milk at room temperatures. Such curdled milk products have been parts of humanity's food treasures in all parts of the world since the most ancient times. The formation of partially *coagulated* blood clots is an important aspect of natural healing in cases of bleeding wounds.

Coagulation in the human body applies at the cellular and the physiological organ level. In Wilhelm Reich's concept of the "muscular armoring," a military metaphor, there is congealing of cellular and tissue fluids. Muscle tissue becomes rigid and hard, reflecting emotional rigidity and defensiveness, and difficulty with relaxation. When the muscular armoring is dissolved, as can happen through directed breathing and bodywork, the individual becomes emotionally more present and relaxed, less armored and defensive.

Condensation

Broadly speaking, *condensation* is the process in which matter in the form of a vapor or a gas is transformed into a liquid. Vapors in the upper atmosphere, like clouds, are *condensed* and liquefied as rain drops in the warmer lower layers of the atmosphere closer to Earth.

In the psycho-alchemical metaphor system, vapors and gases are forms of elemental "air," so we can see and say that complex thoughts and images may be *condensed* from the airy mental level. They are given communicative power when charged with feeling (alchemical "water") in poetic imagery or song, such as in the phrase "drowning in my own tears."

In psychoanalysis, *condensation* is the process by which a single thought-form or symbol is invested with the emotional power of a group of ideas. A written work may be *condensed* into a shorter, denser form.

Coniunctio (L.) ("conjunction")

The *conjoining*, connecting or unifying of two disparate states or processes, weaving together two separate entities or patterns into a new, stronger, healthier wholeness.

In astronomy and astrology, two or more planets or points are said to be conjunct when they occupy the same degree of longitude in the zodiac. The Sun and Moon, which symbolize the masculine and feminine in astrology, are conjunct at the New Moon.

In psychophysical yogic alchemy *coniunctio* refers to practices of balancing the dynamic and receptive poles of the multidimensional human energy field. This field is a polarized electromagnetic antenna system, also called the aura, for receiving and transmitting energies of diverse vibrational frequencies in the multiple worlds of reality and consciousness. Whether clothed in the body of a man or woman, the Immortal Spirit and Soul of every human is androgynous.

At the psychophysical and personality levels, the human being manifests as one or the other, male or female, with in-between variations produced by epigenetic, embryonic, and fetal conditions. The conjoining and integration of the masculine animus and feminine anima is the key central process of psychophysical alchemy. One example of *coniunctio* symbolism in alchemical illustrations is images of a hermaphroditic human being — male on the right side and female on the left. Similar images exist in Indian tantric art. This can be seen as a portrayal of the *coniunctio* practice of visualizing the right side of one's body as male and the left side as female.

The classic Indian yoga posture of sitting cross-legged with hands linked in the lap can also be seen as the portrayal of a *coniunctio* practice: the two poles, dynamic and magnetic, are turned inward and balanced along the central axis, rather than being outwardly oriented, as they are in the normal waking state consciousness and in the activities of daily living.

Corrosion

The word *corrosion* stems from the Latin — *corrodere* — to gnaw something to pieces, as if by a rodent. *Corrosion* is the rusting, dissolving, or eating away of a material substance, especially metals. In physical chemistry, rust is *corroded* iron, a degraded form of metal resulting from oxidation. A rusted metal is weakened, brittle, rigid and discolored, without flexibility or shine.

When we may speak of someone's affect or expressed emotional tone in speaking or writing being *corrosive*, this suggests it is spiteful, malicious or malevolent, as if gnawing and biting. It could be seen in forms of literary or artistic criticism as well as everyday conversation. *Corrosion* as a metaphor has generally negative aesthetic connotations.

However, *corrosion* as rust can also be a metaphor for ordinary forgetting with loss of practice. Our word choice and usage in a foreign language we are not using regularly is a kind of "rusting" *corrosion* of our vocabulary in that language.

Diamonds and Rust is the name of a 1975 album and of a song, by Joan Baez in which she used the contrast between the most precious matter and a *corroded* material substance as a poignant metaphor for the highest and lowest aspects of a love affair, once shining and brilliant, and then later turned dull and rigid.

Crystallization

This is the process that transforms a vapor or a liquid to a solid. Drops of water vapor in the extreme cold of the upper atmosphere become ice *crystals* or snow flakes as they descend towards the earth's surface. As they descend even closer to the ground, they can melt or thaw into water as rain.

Crystals are atoms or molecules arranged in regular, periodically repeated symmetrical lattices. Sand consists of silicates with an irregular, amorphous, asymmetrical structure. Sand can be transformed into glass through fire. Psychological *crystallization,* as in the arts, requires the heat of the fire of attention, just as the increasing heat of closeness to earth transforms the snow into rain.

In the context of human consciousness and creativity we may think of *crystallization* as the transformation of a mixed set of beliefs, thoughts, and emotions into a story or poem or invention that expresses the essential core.

Thought-forms are *crystallized* conceptions — *crystallizations* of akashic or etheric molecules that carry meaning. A thought that says "I'm afraid" or "I'm going to hurt you" are thought-forms *crystallized* from fear or hatred analogous to "hate mail".

In the arts, a vision may be received in a dream or moment of inspiration and is then *crystallized* by the artist into a structure — verbal or visual or poetic or musical.

***

Coagulation and *crystallization* are both transformations of a liquid becoming solid, "water into earth," but coagulation or clotting applies at room temperature, as in the formation of yogurt or cheese, and *crystallization* requires higher temperatures to first purify the liquid. The traditional motto "dissolve and coagulate" applies at the level of mixed cellular tissue, like blood and milk at room temperature.

Dissolve and *crystallize* was not identified in traditional alchemy because it applies at the molecular level, in purified substances. *Crystallization* can only occur in purified substances, and so needs purification to precede it.

Elemental Air

One of the traditional four elements that are the mythopoetic foundation of the Graeco-Roman worldview in the pre-scientific era is elemental *air*. A residue of this correspondence in scientific and everyday languages is the term atmosphere — the sphere of atmos (Greek "vapor" or "breath").

At the planetary level, elemental *air* corresponds to winds, clouds and all atmospheric phenomena. Winds are the breathing of planet Earth, vitalizing and refreshing all plant and animal life.

In esoteric teachings there are four levels of consciousness, called "sheaths" or "bodies" of differing density. The least dense of these is the mental level, also called noetic (Greek, *noesis*, "knowing").

In Jung's psychology the teaching of four aspects of the psyche appears in his theory of four functions and four types, with *air* symbolizing the thinking function, and the type in which that function predominates. "Wings of thought" is an expression that reflects that association. "Wind-bag" and "blow-hard" are colloquial expressions suggesting imbalanced emphasis on *air* and mind in communication.

At the human level, *air* is the basis and medium for breathing, speaking and singing, associated with the energy centers and organs of the head, throat and thoracic cavity.

Colloquially, a scene or a person may bring us a "breath of fresh *air*," especially welcome when we are bored or tired. We may be left "breathless with awe" at the sudden appearance of beauty in a person, a performance or a natural landscape. We may speak or hear in a "whisper," conveying either loving intimacy, or malicious gossip. We may recognize an individual or work of art as "inspiring" or "inspired" — metaphorically as coming from the in-breathing of creative genius.

A proverbial expression alluding to impractical fantasizing is "building castles in the *air.*" In Shakespeare's Twelfth Night, alluding to the echoing effect of *air*, one of the characters says, "Halloo your name to the reverberate hills and make the babbling gossip of the *air* cry out." And in Shakespeare's Tempest, the wizard Prospero asserts the final unreality of creative imaginings when he says, "Our revels now are ended. These our actors . . . were all spirits, and are melted into *air*, into thin *air* — like the baseless fabric of this vision."

Elemental Water

At the planetary level, the element *water* corresponds to oceans, tides, lakes, rivers, springs, pools and rain. Three-fourths of the Earth's surface is covered in *water.* An evolutionary systems cosmology based on the work of Vladimir Vernadsky and Teilhard de Chardin proposes a system of concentric spheres around a fiery core — the lithosphere as the sphere of rock, hydrosphere as the sphere of *water,* atmosphere as the sphere of air, and the biosphere as the sphere of life.

Three-fourths of the mass of the human body, too is fluid, and life on Earth is a *water*-based system. The salty chemistry of blood resembles that of sea*water.* Biological tides ebb and flow through the bodies of all animals and plants, in synchrony with the ocean tides, pulled by lunar and solar gravity.

Analogically, rivers and lakes correspond to the arteries, blood vessels, lymph and endocrine systems of the body and rain to the fertilizing and moisturizing of hormones and sexual fluids. Elemental *water* is associated with feelings and emotions and the energy centers of the chest and solar plexus. Alchemists used the expressions aqua permanens, "permanent *water*" and mare nostrum, "our sea," to refer to the *watery,* fluid components of our being.

Numerous colloquial expressions refer to symbolic associations, both positive and negative, between emotions and fluids. We may experience tears of joy and tears of sorrow. We may recognize someone bubbling infectiously with happiness and joy, or dampening our fiery enthusiasm. Someone may be like a wet blanket at a party or social gathering, or stimulating laughter in everyone to the point of tears, or wishy-washy in their indecisiveness. One may shrug off the negative judgments of others like *water* off a duck's back. And we may appreciate a sad blues song that sings of drowning in my own tears.

We recognize a deep psychological truth in the traditional saying that "you can lead a horse to the *water*, but you can't make him drink." Shakespeare refers to the important difference between surface feeling and depth of emotions, when a character in Henry VI, says "smooth runs the *water* when the brook is deep." Here too, the meaning is both positive and negative: the surface may be calm but conceal hidden rocks or dangerous cross-currents.

Elemental Fire

In the pre-scientific, earth-centered world view of ancient and medieval times in Europe *fire* was one of the traditional four elements that constituted all of reality, along with air, water, and earth. The modern scientific worldview recognizes an evolving and expanding list of some 118 fundamental elements, with known atomic structure. In addition it recognizes the fiery core of planetary structure, which science has penetrated only to a limited extent.

The four elements remain as colloquial symbols in literature and everyday language. The traditional symbolism of *fire* extends to terrestrial *fires* such as lightning, erupting volcanoes and forest *fires*. More broadly it includes all forms of radiant energy, along the entire electro-magnetic spectrum, cosmic radiation and various forms of bio-electricity.

In the human organism, *fire* is experienced as bodily heat and vitality, the electro-chemical activity of the nervous systems and bio-electrical fields involved in healing and regeneration. This includes the various formulations of subtle life-energy processes, such as chi, prana, kundalini, orgone, bioenergy and others.

As psychophysiological metaphor, *fire* and flames are associated with ardor, sexual passion, anger, excitement, vitality, inspiration, vision, imagination, and intuition. All of these states and experiences are linked to the functions and structures of the neuro-endocrine systems, as well as the subtle energy fields and the chakras.

Elemental Earth

The *earth* elements at the planetary/cosmic levels are the rocks, minerals, mountains, deserts, crystals, soil, vegetation, trees, roots — everything tangible with weight and substance. At the level of the human being this includes the living flesh and bones, muscles and other tissues, the skin, the hands and feet, and the sensory awareness associated with these structural organ and cell systems. Where air is associated with mind, water with feeling, fire with perception and intuition, *earth* is associated with sensation, sensitivity and sensuality — again everything tangible that can be weighed, held, and touched. *Earth* is the densest, heaviest, most solid of the four elemental states, what we ordinarily think of when say "matter." The alchemists say, "Elemental *earth* is like a sponge, and the receptacle of all the other elements.

Gold (*aurum nostrum* (L.), "our gold")

Gold, as a precious metal, is traditionally used for coinage and regarded as a medium for the store of value, as well as being crafted for artistic expression in jewelry and ornamentation. The alchemists associated *gold* with the cosmic father principle, and visualized its microcosmic source as a *golden* dome-shaped crown on the chakra above the top of the head. This dome-shaped crown can be seen portrayed in various paintings and sculptures in both Western religious and Buddhist iconography. In the practice of alchemical yoga, the energy from the *golden* crown pours, liquid-like, down and throughout the head and entire body. It has a protective quality and can generally transform negative and depressing energy in the mind-body persona into a positive, protective, and uplifting aura.

The Grail or Graal

Searching for the Holy *Grail* was a metaphor for the spiritual quest that arose in the late middle Ages, in association with knighthood and the path of the warrior. The *grail* knights dedicated themselves to fighting for their king or lord, or for the favor of a noble lady or queen. In the legends of the *grail* quest outer journeys and battles are described, but when the natural landscape of the tales changes to a magical one, this indicates that we are in a realm of heightened consciousness.

A variation on the *grail* search occurs in the *Parsifal* of Wolfram von Eschenbach (12th C.). In this version of the story, the *grail* or *graal* was said to be not a cup but an immaculate, celestial stone — *lapis excoeilis*, a stone from heaven, which had the magical power to heal all ailments and restore one's youth. The knights of the *grail* or graal legends, searching for the cup or the stone, wandered dejectedly through the "grey lands," finding in the desolate wilderness of dim light and sparse vegetation at first no clues and no hope in their search. Two of the knightly fraternity, Gawain and Parsifal, finally find the Castle of Marvels. With its moving furniture and visible angels this is clearly an inner place, filled with spirits that provide both healing and also riches to those who can pass the test and ask for spiritual guidance or assistance.

The test that many knights attempted but failed until Gawain and Perceval passed, was that to be healed and to win the favor of a lady they had to stop fighting, whether for their liege/lord or a noble lady, and ask the question of meaning — what is it I am actually seeing here, among these extraordinary and marvelous appearances? Who are my guides and allies, and who are actually the enemies I am committed to fighting?

Having found the miraculous vision stone, Parsifal was granted access to the hidden castle where the wounded Fisher King was lying in unending torment. Uttering the fundamental words of compassion, "What ails you?" magically opened the gates of the castle, and allowed Parsifal to heal the wounded king, restoring the blighted wastelands to fertility and prosperity.

The Green Lion: Purificatio

The Green Lion Eats the Sun - at the level of individual yogic practice this aphorism refers to the practice of purificatio: when you "*eat*" the *Sun*, you have fire in your belly; your psychometabolism is cooking in the abdominal cauldron.

At the planetary level the "*green lion*" is a hybrid symbol of plant and animal life, "*eats*" means consumes and transforms, "*Sun*" means "solar energy". Modern science confirms the alchemists' insight: solar energy influx to planet Earth is harnessed by plants to build vegetative matter using chlorophyll, and then animals including humans *eat* these plants. So the statement is a condensed symbol of the basic biospheric ecosystem, which is sustained by solar energy through the symbiotic combination of plant and animal life

Lapis philosophorum, (L.)

Searching for the philosophers' Stone is the central metaphor of the alchemical tradition. By examining the alchemists' mysterious utterances about the *lapis*, we can gain some sense of the meanings hidden in their paradoxical metaphors.

Lapis as stone is matter from the mineral realm, the primordial substance or ground of life, more basic even than cellular and organic life. The symbolism of stone refers both to the immobility of the body and stillness of the mind in a meditative "stoned" state.

The *lapis* was also said to be fluid, like an essence or tincture, or a combination of stone and water, as in a text called "The Waterstone of Wisdom" (*The Sophic Hydrolith*). Thus it is a state of consciousness that is solid and still, but also nonattached and flowing, like "the watercourse way" of the ancient Chinese Taoist masters.

This *lapis* stone was said to be everywhere around in external reality, and yet not obvious and overt. "Our stone is openly displayed before the eyes of all, and yet it is not known." In other words this water-stone consciousness is not a specific object "out there" but a function of the subjective attitude and perspective we adopt.

"Our Stone is found in all mountains, all trees, all herbs, all animals and all human beings." In other words, the *lapis* is a shared subjective quality ("our Stone") combined with an objective perception ("found in all mountains").

The "Stone" is within: "This thing is extracted from you, you are its ore." It is a state of consciousness that can only be known by personal experience, the ability to be objective about the "hard facts" of a given situation as it actually is, without subjective illusions or distortions.

This is the crux of the paradoxical and elusive nature of the *lapis* as an experience and its relation to language. When we know truth, we know it, at least for that moment or situation. But truth, as we also understand, is elusive and hard to capture in language, especially when dealing with multidimensional experience. So we resort to paradox, symbol and metaphor — we say it's solid, like rock, and yet fluid like water. We say it's hidden, like a secret, but also obvious and open for all to see.

Massa confusa (It.)

("confused or mixed-up mass")

Normal everyday state of consciousness. The beginning stage of the alchemical process of transformation, when the elements of our psychic constitution — our thoughts, feelings, sensations and impulses — are a jumbled disordered mass, without a coherent center or direction. Through the processes of the alchemical *opus* (work), our mixed thought-feeling-sensation complexes may be sorted and rearranged into ordered geometric patterns, like crystals. These could be as squares, trines, conjunctions and oppositions depicted in the geometric arrangements of the planets in a horoscope at any given time — which seems to have been Kepler's idea.

Mortification (L. *mortificatio*)

Being *mortified* is to experience shame, humiliation or wounded pride. It has echoes of monastic practices and self-flagellation, supposedly designed to reduce the power of ego and pride, creating a sense of humiliation and a defeated ego. But the alchemist's intentional *mortification* is not self-flagellation or wallowing in guilt. It is recognizing your own limitations or your own nothingness in relationship to your divine potential. It means acknowledging your limitations in comparison to your potentials. Gurdjieff used to say only when you realize that you, your ego, is nothing, a nobody, i.e. completely "dead", then you can start to actually grow into someone with real consciousness.

Natura naturans (L.)

This is a core guideline for all kinds of alchemical work of healing and transformation: "nature is doing everything naturally." We only need to tune in and follow her guidance, our natural body-mind. This principle is also expressed in the idea that the body heals itself, and the Taoist principle of "going with the flow" and the concepts of the primal, wild, instinctual, or indigenous mind. Some speak of it as "first nature," distinguishing from "second nature," which refers to acquired automatic habits that we perform unconsciously, like driving, or getting dressed, or regular eating, etc.

Nigredo (Sp.) ("dense darkness")

The dark place of depression, when everything seems dense, obscure and heavy. The "black mood," melancholia, when one feels stuck in obstacles and frustrations. Ordinary objects in the environment and other people appear visually *dark*, as if covered in dark gauze, and look downcast, heavy as if carrying a burden — as indeed they are. There is no fixed rule about how long the *nigredo* as a depressed state of consciousness lasts — it could be days, months, or years, and it can also vary cyclically, as in manic-depressive disorders. It depends on how much intentional healing work you bring to bear on yourself. For the alchemist, this can be the starting point of the transformative process, when you seek help to get out of the black despair, either through psychotherapy, or through intentional inner-directed work. If left untreated, the black depressed states can lead to suicide. Ernest Hemingway used the image of a black dog for his depressive, suicidal episodes.

Opus and Opus contra naturam

Opus (L.) ("the work")

The *work* of self-transformation is on the physical, perceptual, emotional and mental dimensions of consciousness. The process of self-transformation to higher consciousness doesn't happen accidentally or spontaneously by itself — although there may be unexpected peak experiences, or moments of "gratuitous grace." But for ongoing radical self-transformation towards higher consciousness, we need intention and we need practice, which is of course a creative work. In the realm of musical creation, "opus" is used to designate the sequence of a composer's creative output, arranged in chronological order. In the alchemical *opus* of self-transformation, we are both the composer and the performer, and the processes we engage in are arrayed along the time-line of our lives. So the *opus* of our youthful years may be decidedly different than the *opus* of our later years.

Opus contra naturam (L.)

This is a second core motto of the alchemical work: "working against nature" refers to conscious intentional work against the inertial pull of unconscious habits. This is a core principle of practice in "fourth way" teachings such as those of Zen Buddhism, Sufism, Gurdjieff and others.

Osmosis

In chemistry, *osmosis* is the diffusion between two bodies of fluids, a movement from more concentrated to less, through a semi-permeable membrane until the fluid is of an equal concentration on either side of the membrane. In the metaphorical language of alchemy, *osmosis* is any gradual, often unconscious, process of assimilation or absorption that resembles diffusion. For example, the loving partner of a man or woman speaking a different language may gradually absorb elements of the foreign language by semi-conscious *osmosis*. Perhaps an attitude or practice of self-awareness can also be learned in this way.

Sympathy is unconscious affective contagion and empathy as intentional affective resonance is analogous to *osmosis* — spreading from one person's emotional center to another one or more. The "membrane" is the armoring of the emotional energy field.

Feeling states are received and transmitted through diffusion and transfusion directly from one person's emotional body-field to one or more others. For example, in crowds at a pop concert the feelings of admiration/love for the performer is spread by *osmosis* through the entire audience at the dance hall. In classical music concerts, this bonding of energy fields is broken off by the clapping at the end of a performance.

Ourobouros (Gk.) ("tail-swallowing serpent")

This image portrays a *serpent* in circular form with its tail-end in its mouth. This portrays an alchemical energy current. A flow of reddish-gold energy is directed to flow from a point below the upper lip down the front of the body, between the legs at the genitals and then up along the spine, back of the neck, over the top of the head and down the center of the face, reconnecting with the current there and making a complete circuit. The current integrates the three energy fields of the head-throat, the lungs-heart and the abdomen-pelvis in a continuous circulating current.

Precipitation

Water droplets or ice condense from water vapor, sufficiently massive to fall as rain or snow crystals. The weather forecast may say — "we will have heavy *precipitation* today." The atmospheric element air becomes condensed into elemental water through a drop in temperature and becomes sufficiently heavy to fall as rain. If the rain water *precipitates* down to even colder layers closer to earth it solidifies as snow crystals. More generally, a *precipitate* is a solid or solid phase chemically separated from a solution. We also know the metaphorical meaning of *precipitate* and *precipitous* as rash actions and fast downward movements, like falling from a *precipice* or other height. With all these meanings a physical process or solid matter comes downward, falls, from the realm of thought or feeling, where intentions originate, into the time-space realm of action

Prima materia (L.) (The "prime matter")

In alchemy this is the starting point and physical basis of the self-transformative work or *opus*. It is the physical substance of the body, with its bones and nerves and muscles as well as habit patterns and traits. In yoga, as in alchemy, the work and practices with the physical body posture, diet, movement, breathing is not only the starting area of the transformative work, but also its continuing basis. As you work with the higher-frequency levels — perceptual, emotional, and mental — you are continuing with the transformation of the *prima materia*.

Probability and Possibility

The *probabilities* of various events, outcomes and occurrences, both in our personal lives and in the world can be calculated according to the mathematics of *probability*. According to this principle the *probability* of various events occurring in the future are calculated on the basis of how frequently they have occurred in the past. Even the *probabilities* of rare events, such as earthquakes, are estimated and calculated because of their significant potential impact. Such estimates are commonly used in weather forecasting, stock market prices, sales projections, insurance actuarial tables, health and medical prognosis, educational curricula, and journalistic predictions about public events and personalities.

The projections do not assume or imply a causal relationship — the connection between past and future events is acausal, i.e., no causality is stated or implied. Public forecasts of weather patterns, for example, may incorporate speculations about wind, ocean currents and other deeper events that are assumed to be underlying causes of the predicted likely outcomes.

Possibilities relate to personal vision: they represent the subjective experience and personal interest of the person who is having the vision. *Possibility* is the basis of all invention, innovation, and discovery in both technology and art. *Possibilities* cannot be quantified, but compared to the calculus of *probability* they represent an enormous, almost infinite, range of conceivable outcomes.

The indeterminate web of *possibilities,* which can be explored, but not predicted precisely, represents an enormous expansion of consciousness, compared to the quantifiable calculus of *probabilities.* Visions of *possibilities* occur at the intersection of subjective experience and objective reality.

Purificatio (L.) ("purification")

The core process of physical and psychic alchemy, a necessary preparation and accompaniment of all the other processes of transformation. The overlays, crusts and coverings over our patterns of perception, emotion and thought are like the rigidified muscles and bones on the physical level, the sticky swamps in the emotional nature or the foggy cobwebs in the attics of the mind. They need to be burned off with the fires of *purification* to permit the inherent pristine beauty, clarity, flexibility, and radiance to become apparent.

Quartz Crystal SiO$_2$

A vitreous mineral substance, silicon dioxide (SiO$_2$), found worldwide, is a component in sandstone and granite, agate, chalcedony, chert, flint, and opal. It also occurs in pure transparent crystalline form ("crystal *quartz*") in rock crystal, and in mineralized zones. It is the starting point, the *prima materia*, for making instruments of enhanced perception — such as telescopes and microscopes. The amorphous *quartz* is melted, refined, polished, refined, and cut to precise refractive indices. The alchemists valued *quartz* crystals and considered their transparency a sign that it is a highly evolved member of the mineral kingdom. The use of a *crystal* magnifying glass to focus sunlight to ignite a fire in dry matter was evidence of its unique power. In modern times, silicon crystals (still SiO$_2$) are key components of integrated circuits in the digital world.

Quintessence (L. *quintessentia* – "fifth essence")

The highly concentrated and purified essence of something. This is an alchemical metaphor that has migrated into everyday language. A kind of synthesis of the four other elements — each being somehow solid, fluid, vapor-like and fiery-electric. The *quintessence* is not perceptible by ordinary perception, but perhaps accessible to some kind of synaesthesia. Some alchemists said if air, water, fire and earth correspond to the personality layers of thought, feeling, perception and physicality, the *quintessence* then would be like soul, the higher frequency dimension that has aspects of each of these four layers. In Indian yogic alchemy, the fifth element was called *akasha*, usually translated as "ether" — also thought of as a subtle synthesis of the other four.

Rubedo ("the redness" (L.), *rubidus,* red)

Rubedo is another phase or state of consciousness in the three-stage process of alchemical self-transformation, with albedo and nigredo. These mood phases do not necessarily appear in an invariant sequence, but may oscillate back and forth over periods of days, weeks, or months. It may be a matter of long-term mood proclivities when we say of someone they have a "fiery temper," given to outbursts of high drama and rage. In the modern psychiatric terminology, this relates to the manic phase of manic-depressive episodes.

In the fiery *rubedo* phase or state of consciousness you are typically involved with and connected to the heart-felt stirrings of your emotional nature. Your heart may be filled with storms and outbursts, or the pouring rain of tears and anguish, or the passionate intensity of sexual encounters as well as the calmer but warm emotions of friendship and conviviality. This stage too may last months or years or a whole lifetime. Its intentional and controlled expression may be the foundation of your career if you are an actor or actress in theatre or film. Connected to the masculine life cycle this is the phase of the *vir rubeus* (the *red* man).

You are in the *rubedo* phase when you work with the purifying fires and focus your attention and your intentional process on the Sun in the heart-center. You are then walking on what Native American traditions call the "*red* road of life."

Separatio (L.) (separating)

Analogous to the practices of analytical chemistry, *separatio* is a key process in alchemy, akin to psychoanalysis and to shamanic practices of dismemberment. The strands or threads (*samskaras*) of thoughts, feelings, inner and outer perceptions, etc., are set apart, like the complex patterns of a tapestry we are weaving — so we can *separate*, track and analyze the personal, the ancestral, the karmic and the prenatal threads of our mental, emotional and perceptual nature. In the alchemical literature the *separatio* process is practiced alternating repeatedly with the *coniunctio* process. The *separatio* is akin to analysis and adopting a separate point of view for clearer analysis.

In creative performances, the members of a quartet of musicians will practice "playing" each of their "parts" *separately* and alternate that with practicing together as a group or partnership.

Separatio can have either positive or negative implications for growth and healing. In psychoanalysis, *separating* and identifying different complexes can be an essential component of diagnosis.

In medicine, *separatio* can refer to the correct analysis of the different molecular elements of a disease process, which may require microscopic analysis of blood and other bodily fluids.

Silver   (*argentum nostrum* (L.), "our silver")

Silver, the precious metal, has numerous uses in society — as coinage and store of value, or as a medium for artistic expression in jewelry and personal wear. Because it can be tarnished and also exists in greater abundance, *silver* is considered less valuable than gold in commerce and coinage. In alchemical yoga, *silver* light-fire energy is associated with the cosmic mother archetype. It is visualized in the form of a *silver* chalice located about 6" above the crown of the head, from where the fluid *silvery* energy can pour down throughout and around the entire body and energy field. The *silver* energy as an experience is described as having a nurturing, healing, and comforting quality. It can also be experienced as fierce maternal protection — as it is well known that a mother mammal is the most dangerous animal to anyone threatening to harm its offspring. In the alchemical yoga practice, the offspring would be the mind-body persona of the practitioner.

Solutio (L.) (dissolving)

The process of reducing solids to fluids, as in melting and disintegrating a mix of two or more component solid substances. An image or dream vision can vanish and *dissolve*; a meeting of people on a project or a parliament can be *dissolved*; a person may *dissolve* emotionally with tears in their eyes; an image in a photo or film may *dissolve* and change into another one. The traditional alchemical prescription — *solve* et coagula — "*dissolve* and coagulate" was saying: practice *dissolving* the rigid defensive patterns and coagulating or congealing new and healthier and fluid emotions into flexible patterns of thought and behavior.

A new alchemical prescription — *dissolve* and crystallize — is saying: *dissolve* the old defensive emotion-thought defensive patterns and re-crystallize the purified energy essences, bringing more awareness and pure intention into the forms of mind and behavior. Gurdjieff talked about "premature crystallizations," that may have to be *dissolved* and re-formed again and again, since they may hold immature thought forms from an earlier time of your life, and are no longer appropriate.

Sublimatio (L.) ("sublimating")

In chemistry to *sublimate* a substance is to transform it from a solid form to a gaseous state, without passing through a liquid state. In psychoanalysis to *sublimate* an impulse is to bring it into creative not destructive expression — a sexual attraction or desire may be *sublimated* into artistic expression in poetry, music or dance, an aggressive drive may be *sublimated* in a competitive sport, like tennis or football. In the practice of alchemical yoga, *sublimatio* would involve the practice of raising the psychophysical energy-flow of attention and expression from the centers in the lower abdomen and pelvis to the centers in the heart-field, throat and head. *Sublimation* is also involved when the erotic drive is *sublimated* from the personal to the transpersonal and spiritual dimensions, as in the poetry and music of the Sufi mystics and medieval troubadours.

Synchronicity.

C. G. Jung, as a psychologist, writing from within the standard scientific paradigm, called *synchronicity* an "acausal connecting principle" in which events are linked by *meaning* rather than by causality. This is the principle underlying mantic, oracular procedures such as calculating the astrological birth chart, laying out the tarot cards, consulting the Chinese Taoist *I Ching*, or the Nordic runes. You approach the oracle with a personal question in mind — the layout of the oracle chosen according to one of traditional methods then provides an answer to your question. This "answer" then still needs to be interpreted as it applies to the specifics of your situation or question.

A deeper perspective from esoteric physics regards *synchronicity* as the more basic principle and causality as a special case connection which fits within the Western paradigm of causality. Cause-effect connections are linear, local, and occur within the Newtonian time-space paradigm. *Synchronic* connections are multi-dimensional and non-local and involve conscious intention and/or a question. Causal connections occur, according to the laws of physics, whether or not someone sees or recognizes them. *Synchronicities* only occur when consciously recognized by someone and thus represent a unique connection between objective reality and subjective experience.

Notes & References

1. The Freemasons had members of their brotherhood among the founding fathers of the American nation. They left one of their secret insignia, an eye enclosed in a triangle, on that most universal American artifact, the dollar bill.

2. *The Hermetic Museum*, restored and enlarged, trans. from the Latin (London: James Elliot & Co., 1893; orig. publ., Frankfort: 1678). Introduction by A. E. Waite. This is one of the outstanding anthologies of later alchemical texts, mostly anonymous, published in English in a limited edition of two hundred and fifty copies. The sentence quoted is found in volume 2, p. 183. Jung gives extensive quotations from this and other alchemical anthologies not accessible to this writer. Hence, his five books on alchemy are the many reference source used here, besides the work mentioned above.

3. "The Ordinal of Alchemy," *Herm. Mus.*, vol. 2, p. 12.

4. Carl Jung, *Memories, Dreams and Reflections* (New York: Vintage Books, 1961), p. 205.

5. *Ibid.*, p. 221.

6. *Ibid.*, p. 205.

7. Carl Jung, *Alchemical Studies*, vol. 13, *Collected Works* (New York: Pantheon Books, Bollingen Series XX 1967), p. 138.

8. *Herm. Mus.*, vol. 1. p. 108.

9. "An Open Entrance to the Closed Palace of the King," Herm. Mus. vol. 2 p. 183.

10. "The Only True Way," *Herm. Mus.*, vol. 1, p. 155.

11. "A Demonstration of Nature," *Herm. Mus.*, vol 1, p. 130.

12. "The Glory of the World or Tables of Paradise," *Herm. Mus.*, vol. 1, p. 210.

13. Jung, *Alchemical Studies*, p. 73.

14. *Ibid.*, p. 86.

15. "The New Chemical Light," *Herm. Mus.*, vol. 2, p. 131.

16. Rodney Collin, *The Theory of Celestial Influence* (London: Stuart, 1954), p. 151.

17. "The New Chemical Light," *Herm. Mus.*, vol. 2, p. 136.

18. *Herm. Mus.*, vol. 2. p. 64.

19. *Herm. Mus.*, vol. 1. p. 198.

20. "A Demonstration of Nature," *Herm. Mus.* vol. 3, p. 135.

21. "The New Chemical Light," *Herm. Mus.,* vol. 2, p. 14.

22. *Herm. Mus.,* vol. 1. p. 158.

23. *Ibid.,* p. 219.

24. Jung, *Alchemical Studies,* p. 137.

25. *Herm. Mus.,* vol. 1. p. 153.

26. "Glory of the World," *Herm. Mus.,* vol. 1, p. 210.

27. Quoted in Carl Jung, *Mysterium Coniunctionis,* vol. 14, *Collected Works* (New York: Pantheon Books, Bollingen Series XX, 1963), p. 220.

28. *Herm. Mus.,* vol. 2. p. 175.

29. *Herm. Mus.,* vol. 2. p. 74.

30. *Herm. Mus.,* vol. 2. p. 35.

31. *Herm. Mus.,* vol. 2. p. 143.

32. "The Golden Tract," *Herm. Mus.,* vol. 1. p. 14.

33. Jung, *Mysterium Coniunctionis,* p. 113.

34. *Herm. Mus.,* vol. 2. p. 165.

35. *Ibid.,* p. 107.

36. *Herm. Mus.,* vol. 1. p. 22.

37. Jung, *Mysterium Coniunctionis,* p. 250.

38. *Herm. Mus.,* vol. 2. p. 135.

39. These descriptions were collected by Jung in his essay "The Spirit Mercurius," in *Alchemical Studies,* pp. 191-250.

40. Quoted in Jung, *Mysterium Coniunctionis,* p. 461.

41. "The Golden Tract," *Herm. Mus.,* vol. 1. p. 27.

42. *Ibid.,* p. 33.

43. "An Open Entrance," *Herm. Mus.,* vol. 2. p. 176.

44. Jung, *Mysterium Coniunctionis,* p. 145.

45. "Glory of the World," *Herm. Mus.,* vol. 1, p. 210.

46. Quoted in Carl Jung, "Psychology of the Transference," *Practice of Psychotherapy,* vol. 16, Collected Works (Princeton: Princeton University Press, Bollingen Series XX, 1954), p. 298.

47. Carl Jung, *Aion: Researches into the Phenomenology of the Self,* vol. 9, II, *Collected Works* (Princeton: Princeton University Press, Bollingen Series XX, 1959), p. 167.

48. These drawings and the texts accompanying them are from a text entitled *Rosarium Philosophorum* ("The Rosary of the Wise"), which Jung quotes and uses to illustrate his (to me,

incorrect) thesis that the "conjunction" referred to an external relationship. "Psychology of Transference," pp. 211-270.

49. John Pordage, quoted in Jung, "Psychology of Transference," p. 301.

50. Jung, "Psychology of Transference," p. 288.

51. Gospel According to Thomas (London: Collins, 1959), logos 22.

52. Jung, "Psychology of Transference," p. 286.

54. Jung, "Alchemical Studies" p. 163.

55. "The Sophic Hydrolith," *Herm. Mus.,* vol. 1, p. 77.

56. Gerhard Dorn, quoted in Jung, *Mysterium Coniunctionis,* p. 482.

57. Hortulanus, quoted in Jung, "Psychology of the Transference," p. 204.

58. "Three Treatises of Philateles," *Herm. Mus.,* vol. 2, p. 249.

59. "Glory of the World," *Herm. Mus.,* vol. 1, p. 209.

60. *Ibid.,* p. 209.

61. Jung, *Mysterium Coniunctionis,* p. 51.

62. Morienus, quoted in Jung, *Aion,* p. 166.

63. Russell Schofield, "Agni Yoga as Taught in the School of Actualism" (Los Angeles, 1969)

64. *Herm. Mus.,* vol. 1. p. 210.

65. "The New Chemical Light," *Herm. Mus.,* vol. 2, p. 108.

66. "Glory of the World," *Herm. Mus.,* vol. 1, p. 173.

67. Jung, *Mysterium Coniunctionis,* p. 270.

68. "Glory of the World," *Herm. Mus.,* vol. 1, p. 210.

69. "The New Chemical Light," *Herm. Mus.,* vol. 2, p 141

70. P. D. Ouspensky, *In Search of the Miraculous* (New York: Harcourt, Brace & World, 1949) p. 176.

71. Jung, "Alchemical Studies" p. 135.

72. *Ibid.,* p. 153.

73. Ruthven Todd, "Coleridge and Paracelsus; Honeydew and LSD," *London Magazine* (March, 1967), 52-62.

74. Jung, "Alchemical Studies" p. 160n.

75. Brian Inglis, in his book *The Case for Unorthodox Medicine* (New York: G. P. Putnam's Sons, 1964), p. 98, wrote "Perhaps the most striking confirmation of the homeopathic theory has come out of recent investigation into hallucinogens,

and in particular into LSD." For an account of the action of homeopathic preparations in terms of polymer structures in the fluid component of biological systems, see G. P. Barnard and James H. Stephenson, "Fresh Evidence for a Biophysical Field," in Main Currents of Modern Thought, 24, no. 5 (1968): 115-122. The authors conclude that "what the homeopathic physician is attempting to do is to match the pure quantized informational content of particular chemicals to the informational needs of his patients and, at the same time, to take account of the individual capacity of the patient to process information at a given rate."

76. "Salt," Van Nostran's Scientific Encyclopedia, 4th ed. (Princeton: Van Nostran Co., 1968), p. 1561.

77. *Rosarium Philosophorum* in Jung, "Psychology of Transference," p. 274.

78. "The Book of Alze," *Herm. Mus.,* vol. 1, p. 264.

Ralph Metzner (1936-2019) obtained his Ph.D. in clinical psychology at Harvard University, where he collaborated with Timothy Leary and Richard Alpert on psychedelic research. He authored over 100 articles and more than 20 books, including *Ecology of Consciousness, The Unfolding Self* and *Green Psychology.* He was a psychotherapist in private practice, teacher of Alchemical Divination Training, professor emeritus at the California Institute for Integral Studies in San Francisco and co-founder of the Green Earth Foundation. He lived in Sonoma, California.

Cathy Coleman obtained her Ph.D. in East-West psychology from the California Institute of Integral Studies (CIIS) where she served as a senior administrator for over two decades, and currently works with the Center for Psychedelic Therapies and Research at CIIS. She was Executive Director of EarthRise Retreat Center at the Institute of Noetic Sciences, and President of Kepler College, a Washington state-approved college in astrological studies, and co-founder of the Green Earth Foundation. She works in private practice as an astrologer and coach, and writes a weekly blog, *In the Stars.*

www.ingramcontent.com/pod-product-compliance
Lightning Source LLC
Chambersburg PA
CBHW032056040426

42335CB00036B/421